Nurture Groups
in School and at Home

Nurture Groups in School and at Home

Connecting with Children with Social, Emotional and Behavioural Difficulties

**Paul Cooper
and Yonca Tiknaz**

Foreword by Marion Bennathan

**Jessica Kingsley Publishers
London and Philadelphia**

First published in 2007
by Jessica Kingsley Publishers
116 Pentonville Road
London N1 9JB, UK
and
400 Market Street, Suite 400
Philadelphia, PA 19106, USA

www.jkp.com

Copyright © Paul Cooper and Yonca Tiknaz 2007
Foreword copyright © Marion Bennathan 2007

Library of Congress Cataloging in Publication Data
A CIP catalog record for this book is available from the Library of Congress

British Library Cataloguing in Publication Data
A CIP catalogue record for this book is available from the British Library

ISBN 978 1 84310 528 2

Printed and bound in Great Britain by
Athenaeum Press, Gateshead, Tyne and Wear

This book is dedicated to the memory of Marjorie Boxall, the founder of nurture groups, and to Marion Bennathan who continues to be a fearless champion of nurture groups through her role as founder and chair of the Nurture Group Network.

Acknowledgements

The authors would like to thank the Calouste Gulbenkian Foundation for the financial support that helped make the writing of this book possible, and the patient attention of Stephen Jones and Karin Knudsen at Jessica Kingsley who made sure we finished the book. We would like to thank Marion Bennathan and Jim Rose of the Nurture Group Network (NGN) for help and support. Their enormous experience, knowledge and wisdom has been invaluable to us. We are particularly grateful to them for sharing with us evaluation data that has been lodged with the NGN by many of its members. We wish to give a special thanks to those Nurture Group practitioners who gathered this data and gave permission to the NGN to use it in this way. We would also like to thank Ray Arnold and Eve Boyd, who have contributed to the collection and analysis of some of the data drawn on in the book. We are confident in saying that Eve and Ray have trained more teachers and teaching assistants than anyone anywhere. Therefore, they have to take a significant slice of the credit for the burgeoning success of Nurture Groups throughout the UK and beyond. David Whitebread has also played a vitally important role in some of our data analysis and conceptual work. There would of course be nothing to write about were it not for excellent work of the many teachers and teaching assistants who work in Nurture Groups and mainstream classrooms. We would like to thank all of these people, and especially those who have participated in our various studies. Thanks also to the support given by Barbara Blatherwick of Braunstone Community Action, in Leicester, Amanda Hart, Alison Bradley, and Michelle King of the City of Leicester SEN Teaching Service, and the numerous Nurture Group staff and other school staff in Leicester's rapidly growing range of Nurture Group provision. Last, but by no means least, we wish to express our gratitude to the children and parents who have generously given their time to our research.

Paul Cooper and Yonca Tiknaz

Contents

List of Tables

List of Figures

Series Editor's Foreword

The twin needs to raise educational standards for all and to improve access to educational opportunities for the most vulnerable members of society continue to be major challenges facing educators throughout the world. The persistent link between socio-economic status and educational attainment is one of the few truly dependable outcomes of social scientific research. Children who come from socially deprived backgrounds are at much greater risk of educational failure than children who come from more privileged backgrounds. In the USA, in 1979 individuals from the top income quartile were four times more likely to successfully complete a four-year college degree programme than individuals from the bottom quartile (ETS 2005). By 1994 the disparity had increased from 4 to 10 times (*ibid.*). In the UK similar concerns have been noted by the DfES (2004). There is a further association between educational failure and social, emotional and behavioural difficulties (*ibid.*), as well as an association between social, emotional and behavioural problems and social disadvantage (Schneiders, Drukker, Ende *at al.* 2003).

The interaction between socio-economic, educational and socio-emotional factors is clearly complex and multi-faceted. It is certainly not the case that any one of these factors necessarily precedes either of the others. Resilience factors of various kinds come into play for some people, enabling them, as individuals, to buck the statistical trends. Temperament, social and cognitive strategies, personal values, external social support structures, and parental personality characteristics, can help to create opportunities for unpredicted positive educational and socio-emotional outcomes for individuals who appear to be in the most dire socio-economic circumstances (Rutter 1987). Unfortunately, there are counterbalancing risk factors, which will combine with disadvantage for other people to create serious life problems (e.g. Patterson, Reid and Dishion 1992).

It is all too easy to place the blame for a child's educational failure and disruptive behaviour on family and/or neighbourhood factors, and to write off whole geographical areas as being populated by 'undesirables'. It is perhaps because of the dangers of provocative, negative stereotyping of this kind that we sometimes neglect the socio-economic correlates of educational disengagement and social, emotional and behavioural difficulties.

A crucial factor that can be both a cause and effect of educational failure is what David Smith, in the Edinburgh Study of Youth Transitions and Crime, describes as 'attachment to school' (Smith 2006). Attachment to school can be defined in terms of the degree of commitment towards and engagement with schooling that students feel. Students who have a strong attachment to school have feelings of attachment to teachers, and believe that success in school will lead to significant rewards in later life. Weak attachment to school is characterised by indifference or hostility towards teachers and scepticism about the value of schooling. Weak attachment to school can lead to disaffection and alienation. These are problems of a psychological nature that impair the individual's capacity for social and academic engagement that can, in turn, lead to reduced life chances.

Innovative Learning for All offers a series of publications each of which considers ways in which schools in the 21st century can address the needs of vulnerable students and contribute to their effective attachment to school and engagement with educational opportunities. Each author in the series offers insights into different ways in which these goals can be achieved by drawing on the best available, and in some cases original, research evidence. At the heart of the series is the shared view that educational standards for everyone will improve if we focus our efforts on promoting the educational engagement of the most vulnerable. There is also a strong consensus around the need to value all children and young people as individuals and to maintain a commitment to their positive growth, and for these values to be translated into practical support that is informed by a firm conceptual and technical understanding.

This is not to say that education is a cure all for the dysfunctions of society. Far from it, the ideas and practices described in this series depend upon political will and government action to achieve their best. On the other hand, the programmes and approaches dealt with in this series will not be made redundant by enlightened and effective measures that address social and economic deprivation. However, they will, undoubtedly, be aided by such measures. It follows, therefore, that the authors in this series all hope that some of the ideas that they put forward will contribute to both the thinking and practice of educators as well as politicians.

Paul Cooper, University of Leicester

REFERENCES

Barton, Paul E. (1997) *Towards Inequality: Disturbing Trends in Higher Education.* Available online at www.ets.org/portal/site/ets, accessed 29 January 2007.

DfES (2004) *Breaking the Cycle.* London: DfES

Patterson, G., Reid, J. and Dishion, T. (1992) *Anti-Social Boys*, vol. 4. Eugene, OR: Castalia.

Rutter, M. (1987). Psychosocial resilience and protective mechanisms. *American Journal of Orthopsychiatry 57*, 3.

Schneiders, J., Drukker, M., van der Ende, J., Verhulst, J., van Os, J. and Nicolson, N. (2003) Neighbourhood socio-economic disadvantage and behavioural problems from late childhood into early adolescence. *Journal of Epidemiology and Community Health 57*, 699-703.

Smith, D. (2006) *School Experience and Delinquency at Ages 13 to 16.* Edinburgh: Centre for Law and Society, University of Edinburgh.

Foreword

All developed societies are realising with some alarm that in a world where technology has greatly reduced the number of unskilled jobs available to the poorly educated, good educational systems are of paramount importance. In England there has been massive investment in the government policy, Every Child Matters; likewise in the US in the policy of No Child Left Behind. In spite of this there continues to be great concern about poor attainments, about school morale, about high rates of young people virtually dropping out of school, with all the likely consequences of increased criminality, higher incidence of mental illness, and of family problems. It then becomes tempting for legislators to become more controlling of schools, to demonise those young people who are seen, often with justice, as anti-social, to scapegoat parents as not caring about education.

This is not a reality recognisable to those of us with long experience of work with troubled children whether in education, in mental health, in public care or in provision for young offenders. What we see so often is young people hurt, emotionally damaged, depressed, unconfident, angry, feeling they have no place in the world. We also see bewildered parents who wish things had been different, teachers who give so much, often with so little reward. And what we know is that this failure was often predictable and preventable if we all understood the realities of childhood and what children need to succeed in life. It is therefore a great pleasure to me to introduce this book about nurture groups to what should be a wide audience of those concerned for our children.

Nurture groups are a simple, enormously successful early intervention which if widely understood and implemented could do a great deal to help children and young people at risk in our societies. They have the central theme of seeking to understand what the world looks like to the child and then working out the solutions possible in school. Their watchword is 'growth not pathology'. They were the response of Marjorie Boxall to the distress she saw in many young children in Inner London in the 1960s and 70s, and in their teachers and parents. As an educational psychologist, she understood the large numbers being put forward for special education as 'maladjusted' and 'educationally subnormal' as evidence not of inborn deficit but of the failure of the educational system to take account of the child's early development and its influence on their condition at the point of school entry. In *The Nurture Group in the Primary School* (1976, now Chapter 2 in Bennathan and Boxall [2000]) she wrote:

Satisfactory emotional, social and cognitive development in the earliest years is the product of adequate and attentive early nurturing care. It is a many-stranded, intermeshing, forward-moving, unitary learning process that centres on attachment and trust and has its foundations in the close identification of parent and child, and the interaction and participation in shared experiences that stem from this. It is the first stage of a developmental process through which the child builds up adequate concepts and skills, learns to interact and share with others and feel concern for them. Through this process s/he becomes increasingly self-supporting and self-directing and able to profit from the experiences offered at school.

Teachers immediately understood this and with Boxall enthusiastically set up the groups, which as the evidence set out in this book demonstrates were to enhance the lives of many children, their parents, their teachers and their fellow pupils.

Boxall did not see herself as promoting any theoretical stance, rather the influence of early development to her was not a matter of theory but of fact, self-evident and incontrovertible. But the truth is that for academic purists the inner life of the child, the origins of the self we all carry with us throughout life, was not a proper subject for study, not being open to scientific verification or observation. This view is no longer tenable for two reasons.

First there is the work led by John Bowlby. He elucidated the process of the first relationship, the bonding of the child to its carer, showing how this was central to the capacity to relate and so greatly influenced later development, including the capacity to explore the world and to learn. Importantly, he expressed these ideas in ways that could be tested, so ending the scientific disdain that had existed for so long. His work, which came to be called attachment theory, is now widely accepted in the Western world in social work and in mental health work with children and with adults.

Second, there has been a massive leap forward in technology which has made it possible literally to watch what is happening in the brain. It can now be seen that warm attentive care is necessary for optimal development and that when this has been lacking there are gaps in brain development. If the deficit is recognised early and if therapeutic action is taken there is every hope that growth will take place. As these ideas gain ground throughout the English-speaking world the relevance of a project which allows therapeutic attitudes to be embedded centrally in school practice is beginning to be appreciated. Nurture groups are now widespread throughout the UK. There is interest and some development in Canada, in New Zealand and in the US to which, I believe, this timely publication will contribute.

Marion Bennathan, Chair,
Nurture Group Network
February 2007

CHAPTER 1

Nurture Groups

This chapter describes social, emotional and behavioural difficulties and introduces the nurture group concept, describing what it is that nurture groups set out to achieve. It also introduces the basic underpinning assumptions of educational nurturing by exploring the relationship between learning, feelings and behaviour. In other words, this chapter introduces the basics of 'educational nurturing' and gives a brief introduction to some of the issues that are dealt with in more detail later in the book, such as why some children might benefit from being placed in a nurture group.

DEFINING SOCIAL, EMOTIONAL AND BEHAVIOURAL DIFFICULTIES

It is useful to think of social, emotional and behavioural difficulties (SEBD) as an umbrella term incorporating a diverse range of behaviours ranging from 'acting out' behaviours such as aggression, non-compliant behaviour, vandalism and bullying, to 'acting in' behaviours such as social withdrawal, anxiety, depression, extreme passivity, eating disorders, substance abuse and self-harm. Acting out behaviours have a tendency to receive more attention from parents, teachers and the wider community, because they impinge in negative ways on the lives of others. Acting in behaviours, on the other hand, are more likely to be hidden from public view, or even deliberately concealed by an individual. Authoritarian educational and parenting practices can be seen as key contributory factors in the creation and maintenance of both types of SEBD, since acting out behaviours are often modelled on coercive management styles, whilst acting in problems can be fostered in the recipient of such a management style.

One way of thinking about SEBD is in relation to mental health. It is a source of concern that prevalence rates for mental health problems among 11–16-year-olds are increasing. A recent publication by the UK's British Medical Association (2006) estimated that 20 per cent of young people experience a mental health problem at some point in their development, and 10 per cent experience these problems to a level that represents a 'clinically recognisable mental health disorder'. The range of problems includes emotional disorders (such as anxieties, phobias and depression); self-harm and suicide; conduct disorders; hyperkinetic disorders; autistic spectrum disorders; psychotic disorders; eating disorders; and substance and drug abuse. Twenty per cent of this group of young people are diagnosed with two or more disorders.

Of course, SEBD covers more than just mental health problems. Delinquency among young people often overlaps with mental health problems, and both of these major areas seem to relate to adverse social circumstances in the communities where young people live and the schools they attend. The young person who exhibits mental health problems and/or social deviance (including delinquency) is likely to have difficulty in engaging in the school experience and, in the absence of effective intervention, is at great risk of experiencing a deterioration in their presenting difficulties as they move towards and through the adolescent years (Rutter and Smith 1995).

A crucial factor that can be both a cause and effect of SEBD is what David Smith, in the Edinburgh Study of Youth Transitions and Crime, describes as 'attachment to school' (Smith 2006). Attachment to school can be defined in terms of the degree of commitment towards and engagement in schooling that students feel. Students who have a strong attachment to school have feelings of attachment to teachers, and believe that success in school will lead to significant rewards in later life. Weak attachment to school is characterised by indifference or hostility towards teachers and scepticism about the value of schooling.

Weak attachment to school is not necessarily related to mental health difficulties, delinquency or social deviance, but is often a problem in itself that can lead to disaffection and alienation. These are problems of a psychological nature that impair the individual's capacity for social and academic engagement that can, in turn, lead to reduced life chances.

A BRIEF INTRODUCTION TO NURTURE GROUPS

Nurture groups are small classes in infant and primary schools for students with social, emotional, behavioural and learning problems. There are also nurture groups in secondary schools, but these are less common. A 'classic' nurture group has 10 to 12 students, and two staff, a teacher and a teaching assistant. A central aim of nurture groups is to provide students with a secure and safe environment that provides the conditions necessary for them to develop emotionally, socially and cognitively (Boxall 2002). In classic nurture groups, the lessons are highly structured and the nurture group staff ensure a supportive and routinised learning environment within which students' experiences are carefully managed.

The authors of this book view nurture groups as temporarily separated transitional settings which enable students to cope more effectively with the demands of mainstream schooling. Nurture group candidates often present SEBDs which prevent them (and sometimes their peers) from engaging with the schooling experience constructively. Nurture groups are specifically designed to remove or reduce these barriers and therefore to prevent these children from disengaging with the education system in the early stages of their educational history. In addition, nurture groups can have profound and positive effects on whole schools, as well as on relationships within families, such as between carers and children and/or between siblings.

Nurture groups are not a new form of educational provision. They were devised by Marjorie Boxall, an educational psychologist, who set up the first groups in the Inner London Education Authority in the early 1970s (Bennathan and Boxall 2000) in the UK. Having gone through an initial period of popularity, which lasted for the best part of a decade, nurture groups dwindled in numbers, with many of the original groups being closed down (Bennathan and Boxall 2000). In 1998 a national survey found less than 50 groups in the UK (Cooper, Arnold and Boyd 1998). Current (unpublished) evidence (provided by Nurture Group Network in 2006) identifies over 400 groups throughout the UK. This figure reflects only those groups that have registered with the Nurture Group Network. Even at 400, this represents an 800 per cent increase over eight years. Since NGN records show that more than 3000 people have attended four-day award-bearing training courses preparring them to work in nurture groups, the actual number is likely to be much higher.

The possible reasons for this dramatic increase in numbers are complex. At this stage, it is sufficient to say that nurture groups have become a very popular form of provision, both with teachers and carers, at a time when there is considerable concern about the ability of mainstream schools to meet the needs of students with certain special educational needs, SEBD in particular. Changes in educational policy, such as the introduction of national tests for 7, 11 and 13-year-olds, have led to increased pressures in British schools which have been seen to have unfortunate consequences for many young children. Nurture groups appear to offer schools a way of helping children to engage with social and academic aspects of schooling. In turn, they are likely to help students to be more resilient in the face of external pressures such as national testing.

STUDENTS RECEIVE MORE ATTENTION

Nurture groups are specially designed classes that cater for students who are having difficulties in adjusting to the requirements of mainstream classrooms. It is generally believed that students who will benefit most from nurture groups are those who, for whatever reason, have a need for a classroom set-up that allows students to receive more individual attention than is often available in the main-stream classroom. This means that the students each have many opportunities to speak to adults and to get help with their schoolwork. It also means that the adults get to know each student really well. Nurture group staff also engage in intensive interactions with pupils to support them (Nind 1999). These factors combine to help the adults and the students work together in ways that enable each student to get access to experiences that will help him or her develop and improve his or her learning skills, as well as the abilities to understand and manage their feelings and get along with other children.

Some of the children in the nurture group, when they first start attending the group, will be very quiet and withdrawn, whilst others may have a tendency to be excitable and disruptive. Because the members of staff are able to give such close attention to each student, they are able to work hard at getting the quiet students to 'come out of themselves' by engaging them in conversation and designing activities that will gradually help them to feel more comfortable with interacting with other children. They are also able to help students to deal with anger problems and, by observing children carefully, spot the situations which normally lead to disruptive behaviour for specific students. Staff can then prevent disruption from happening. For example, they can do this by teaching the child specific skills for dealing with problem situations (e.g. how to deal with other pupils wanting to borrow equipment), by distracting students from the negative situations (e.g. engaging pupils in an alternative activity whilst the teacher deals with the request to borrow the equipment) and so on. This is not to say that nurture group staff are always successful in preventing students in the nurture group from misbehaving. It would be a very unusual pupil who did not misbehave sometimes. When students in the nurture group misbehave the staff will respond, dealing with the behaviour in ways that are designed to encourage pupils to learn that the best way of getting what they want is to behave in ways that are considerate of other people's feelings.

LINKS BETWEEN LEARNING, FEELINGS AND BEHAVIOUR

Obviously, a key purpose of schooling is to promote students' learning. However, it is increasingly apparent that the kind of learning that is supposed to go on in schools is often undermined by feelings of emotional insecurity that prevent students from concentrating and participating. In fact, nurture groups are built on the principle that the foundations of learning are emotional and social.

A very important feature of the nurture group approach is an understanding of the ways in which the kinds of learning that students are expected to do in schools is closely linked to how they feel about themselves, and how well they are able to get along with other students. It is argued that learning problems, such as difficulties in learning how to read, or problems with understanding numbers, can sometimes be the result of a child's feelings of fear and anxiety which act as a barrier to the child's engagement with the learning task. This reminds us just how stressful the whole business of learning in the classroom can be.

Every time a teacher asks a student to try to carry out a learning activity there is always the possibility that the student will not perform the activity as well as he or she might, or as well as the teacher expects, or as well as other students in the same classroom. We have all been in this situation as children, and we continue to experience similar situations in our adult lives. Although learning new skills can be fun, it can also be very threatening. When we succeed in learning something new it makes us feel good about ourselves. Success breeds success. Once we have succeeded in overcoming one challenge, we have a little more confidence the next time we are confronted with a similar challenge.

Students who benefit most from being in nurture groups are those who seem to have particular difficulty in engaging with classroom learning and getting along with other students in their age group, and who become anxious or angry when in learning situations. The nurture group provides a comfortable and caring environment in which opportunities are given to students that allow them to engage in activities according to their particular level of need. This means that students who have had difficulty in learning how to play will be given the chance to engage in play, at first with an adult, and later with other students and on their own. It is through these experiences that students develop the skills necessary to operate in a classroom group.

In order for students to feel confident about play and work it is important that they feel safe and secure. Nurture group staff work hard to encourage these feelings in their students through the ways in which they talk to the students, and by providing activities that help them develop a sense of belonging to the group. The nurture group room is also specially designed to help students feel comfortable and safe. This is achieved by having all of the features of a normal classroom (e.g. books, desks, whiteboard, computers) along with items that would normally be found in a comfortable home setting (e.g. carpets, soft furnishings, dining table, cooking facilities).

All of these features of the nurture group are directed at helping students feel secure, feel good about themselves, and feel able to work on formal National Curriculum topics and therefore make educational progress. In short, the nurture group sets out to help students develop positive feelings towards school, based on feelings of safety in the school setting; the experience of being cared for by the nurture group staff; the experience of success in getting along with other students; and the experience of achievement in learning activities. All of the time that students are in the nurture group, they are also keeping in close contact with their mainstream class. This prevents nurture group students from developing feelings of exclusion from their mainstream peers. After a relatively short period of time (usually between three and four school terms) they are usually able to return to the mainstream classroom on a full-time basis.

CONCLUSION

A key objective of nurture groups is enabling social and academic engagement. Social and academic engagement can be defined as children's active participation in activities that are designed to promote or secure access to learning in the curriculum. Marjorie Boxall (Bennathan and Boxall 1998) has a very useful concept that helps us understand what is at the heart of nurture groups, when we think about them from a cognitive perspective (Cooper 2005). She refers to the *organisation of experience* which signifies the processes by which students give purposeful attention, participate constructively, connect up experiences, show insightful involvement and engage cognitively with peers. It follows from this that an explicit feature of the organisation of experience concept is social inclusion. Put simply, students become actively engaged in the formal learning activities of the classroom through *social engagement* with others – usually the teachers, teaching assistants and their fellow students. Crucially, this insight reveals to us the inappropriateness of views of teaching and learning that separate cognitive development from emotional development and the social context in which learning takes place. Integral to effective learning in classrooms is the facilitation of appropriate social engagement and the provision of an emotionally supportive environment. The educator brings subject and pedagogical knowledge to the classroom and enables students to access this knowledge through these combined processes. Nurture groups provide a powerful, working illustration of some of the practical implications of these insights.

OUTLINE OF THE BOOK

Chapter 2, A Nurture Group in Action, explores the practical ways in which students can be supported when they are in nurture groups. This includes an account of the organisational features and routines of nurture groups, as well as a discussion of specific features of a nurture group curriculum. In Chapter 3, What School Staff Say About Nurture Groups, we explore the views and experiences that are expressed by adults working in schools about nurture groups. The information for this chapter is based on research carried out in schools which have nurture groups in different parts of the UK. Three important elements of our argument in this chapter are: 1. the need for a whole school commitment to and support for the nurture group, which is based on 2. a shared understanding of the nature and purposes of the nurture group, and 3. the values underpinning the nurture group concept.

Chapter 4, Carers, Children and Nurture Groups, looks at nurture groups from the perspectives of carers who have children in nurture groups, and children themselves. As in Chapter 3, this chapter draws heavily on research carried out in UK schools and the first-hand accounts of carers and children with direct experience of nurture groups. A crucial feature of this chapter is the indication that the nurture group can act as a catalyst in the carer–child relationship, having positive effects which are experienced in the home setting. In Chapter 5, Selection of Students for Nurture Groups, we focus our attention on how students are selected for nurture groups. To explore this, we look at the decision-making process within schools, as well as some of the specific tools that are used to assess students' suitability for nurture groups, such as the Boxall Profile. Emphasis is placed on the importance of consultation and effective communication in the selection process.

Chapter 6, Do Nurture Groups Work? Existing Research on Nurture Groups, examines research evidence that evaluates the effectiveness of nurture groups. The different forms that nurture take are highlighted in this chapter, as well as key factors that influence the effectiveness of different nurture groups. In Chapter 7, Involving Carers in Nurture Groups, we examine the roles that carers can play in helping nurture groups to be effective. It is argued that children often make the best use of opportunities provided by the nurture group if experiences they have outside of the school setting are consistent with the aims and purposes of the nurture group approach. This highlights the importance of the relationship that develops between the carer and the nurture group staff. Where this relationship is positive and based on mutual respect and understanding, children's experiences in the family context will tend to build on and extend the successes that are achieved in the nurture group.

Chapter 8, A Model for Analysing Problem Situations: SALAD, explores a framework developed by Olsen and Cooper (2001) which was designed to analyse problem situations and identify opportunities for intervention. This can be used by both educational professionals and carers. This framework has five key features. These are **S**ystems, **A**ccess, **L**imits, **A**cceptance and **D**irection. The framework is based on the idea that behavioural difficulties often stem from problems in the relationships between carers, children and schools rather than from within individuals. An important objective of the SALAD framework is to identify patterns of interaction between people that create and/or keep problems going, and ways in which these patterns might be altered.

Chapter 9, What Makes a Successful Nurture Group?, looks more closely at some of the key factors that contribute to the success of nurture groups as a form of educational provision. There is always room for improvement in educational interventions. On the basis of research evidence, this chapter focuses on areas that individual schools and nurture groups might consider when seeking to improve the functioning of the nurture group.

In Chapter 10, Key Messages for the Practitioner, we review some of the key ideas that have been explored in the course of the book. Emphasis is placed on the need for schools and carers to work together to provide children with a secure and caring environment that enables them to feel safe and able to engage with the challenges which, in turn, pave the way for healthy social, emotional and intellectual development.

CHAPTER 2

A Nurture Group in Action

In this chapter, we explore the nature of nurture groups in relation to the typical practical arrangements that you would see in a well-run nurture group.

THE CLASSIC NURTURE GROUP

As was noted in Chapter 1, nurture groups have been in existence in the UK since the early 1970s. There are now a number of varieties of nurture groups that differ in important ways from the original model as it was conceived by Marjorie Boxall, the founder of nurture groups. A 'classic' nurture group has 10 to 12 students, and two staff: a teacher and a teaching assistant (TA). It takes students who are already attending mainstream school where the group is located. The students attend the group on usually nine out of ten half-day sessions per week and they remain on the roll of the mainstream class which they attend for registration every morning and one half-day every week. There are now nurture groups in some secondary schools, but these are less common. Most nurture groups are still to be found in infant, junior and primary schools.

In a typical nurture group day, students register with their mainstream class in the morning and are then collected by nurture group staff and taken to the nurture group room. Towards the end of their time in the nurture group (which can last anything between two and four school terms) they will often spend increasingly more time in the mainstream classroom (Boxall 2002). Whilst in the nurture group, students follow a holistic curriculum which is a combination of the formal curriculum (e.g. National Curriculum in England and Wales) and a curriculum which focuses on social and emotional development.

There are differences between nurture groups in terms of how they are set up and how they operate. For example, some nurture groups do not operate for the full nine half-days per week, but may operate on a half-time basis or less. We will explore variations between nurture groups in more detail in Chapter 6. In this chapter, we examine the key characteristics of the classic nurture group, as defined by Marjorie Boxall, the founder of nurture groups, and later developed by Marion Bennathan (Bennathan and Boxall 2000; Boxall 2002). We then examine the Nurture Group Curriculum before finishing with a description of a typical nurture group day.

KEY CHARACTERISTICS OF THE CLASSIC NURTURE GROUP

As we noted in Chapter 1 a central aim of nurture groups is to provide students with a secure and safe environment that provides the conditions necessary for students to develop emotionally, socially and cognitively (Boxall 2002). In classic nurture groups, the lessons are highly structured and the nurture group staff ensure a carefully paced and routinised learning environment, within which students' experiences are carefully managed.

In nurture groups, students are encouraged to value themselves through their experience of being valued and cared for by others (Cooper and Lovey 1999). Opportunities to increase the capacity for understanding and valuing others' feelings are created through activities that are provided and monitored by the nurture group staff (*ibid.*). A key working principle here is the warm and overtly co-operative relationship between the members of the teacher/teaching assistant team. The ways in which they interact with one another publicly provide important social experience for students to observe and imitate. Table 2.1 illustrates a number of working principles of a classic (Boxall type) nurture group.

In the following, we summarise a number of key characteristics of nurture groups.

1. The learning environment in nurture groups

The reason for having a routinised and carefully paced learning environment is so that nurture group students know exactly what to expect every day (Boxall 2002). Nurture groups follow more or less the same routine every day. First, students register with their mainstream class. They are then collected by the nurture group staff, and taken to the nurture group room where they start the day with the same activity (e.g. circle time). At the same point every day, usually halfway through the morning, staff and students prepare and share 'breakfast'. The predictability of the routine helps students to develop secure expectations, which reinforce their sense of emotional security and their sense of trust in the nurture group staff (*ibid.* 2002).

2. The small group size

A classic nurture group usually consists of 10 to 12 students. This is a relatively small group when compared to a mainstream setting. The small group size

Table 2.1: Key working principles of nurture groups

1. The teacher and the TA have very specific roles in creating the nurture group atmosphere

A caring and supportive environment is created by the nurture group teacher and the TA to enable students to develop the skills that they need in order to function in mainstream schooling.

2. The nurture group recreates the process of early learning environment

The structure and content of the nurture group day are appropriate for an early developmental level during the beginning stages, and the teacher ensures a carefully paced and routinised environment within which students' experiences are structured and managed.

3. The nurture group is an integral part of the school in which it is located

It is important that there is close continuity between students' experiences in the nurture group and their experiences elsewhere in the school. This continuity should be happening at the different levels of whole school policies and everyday practices in mainstream classrooms and all other settings throughout the school.

4. The interdependent partnership of the teacher and TA is essential

The nurture group teacher and the TA need to work in an interdependent partnership so that they constitute role-models for students and exemplify constructive interactions.

Based on Boxall 2002

accommodates a number of opportunities that are characteristic of nurture groups. It allows the development of relationships among students and between nurture group staff and students. In this size of group, and with appropriate routines, many opportunities are created to talk about feelings, exchange ideas and listen to others. This can help students to appreciate others' needs and to develop an awareness of others' feelings and emotions.

Having said this, the nurture group is not a substitute for the students' families. The bond developed here is a school one (between school staff and students and among students) for enabling students to develop an attachment to schooling. For this reason, it is important to avoid allowing the number of students in the nurture group to become too small. A group of 10 or 12 students is small enough to allow students to receive individual attention, but is still large enough to require students to see themselves as members of a class group. Nurture group staff exploit this by requiring students to rehearse many of the group activities that are essential to the running of mainstream classes, such as sitting together as a group for story time, lining up when leaving the nurture group, and practising group participation skills such as raising a hand before speaking in class.

Within this small and relatively intimate learning setting, nurture group staff are better positioned to assess students' academic, social and emotional needs. Furthermore, there are more resources available to understand and interpret students' reactions and responses. This allows the nurture group staff to customise their approach to teaching and support the needs of nurture group students more effectively.

The extensive opportunities available for communication afford opportunities for staff to use feedback regularly on how students are progressing in the classroom. Intense communications allow nurture group staff to notice even the smallest elements of progress, for which students can be praised. Conversely, nurture group staff have more opportunities to diagnose and intervene when students experience difficulties in learning, behaviour and in relation to emotional functioning.

One of the key features of the nurture group, from a learning point of view, is the opportunity for flexibility in the structuring and pacing of lessons. For example, in the early stages of being in a nurture group, some students might benefit from some lessons being run at a slower pace that might be the case in typical mainstream classrooms. This means that students are given more thinking time when the teacher or the teaching assistant is conducting whole group question and answer sessions. This is very important because the process of thinking through an answer to a teacher's question, whether or not it produces the right answer, is the key skill that is being developed in these kinds of question and answer situations. If students are not given the time to think their own answers through, then they are not given the opportunity to connect new knowledge with their existing understanding. The making of such connections is central to the process of cognitive development. As students' performance in such tasks improves, the staff can adjust the pace with which lessons are conducted. This is what Bruner and Haste (1987) describe as 'calibration', whereby educators adjust their patterns of engagement with students according to their assessment of students' performance characteristics.

Extensive communication opportunities in nurture groups can greatly help students to develop their self-confidence. Research evidence suggests that students value the opportunity to verbalise their thoughts and opinions and to have these acknowledged by adults and other students (Cooper and MacIntyre 1996). This experience promotes cognitive development and also enhances students' self-esteem and sense of educational empowerment (*ibid.*).

There are students who are much more vocal outside classroom situations than they are within them. This problem can be attributed to the repeated experience of not seeing their potential contributions to the classroom discussions as valid or relevant. In the nurture group situation, staff work hard to encourage students to talk about their thoughts and feelings and offer positive feedback when they do so. As we will see in Chapters 3 and 4, these improvements in nurture group students' self-confidence and willingness to participate are often recognised by mainstream teachers and carers. This suggests that skills of this kind that are developed in the nurture group are transferable to other situations.

3. The nurture group teacher and the teaching assistant working together

Another key feature of nurture groups is the presence of a nurture group teacher and a teaching assistant (TA). The distinctive roles that each plays and how they communicate in the classroom are vital for the success of nurture groups. An important aspect of the relationship is effective role-modelling for students by representing what constitutes positive constructive social interactions and appropriate in-class behaviour. Such interactions and behaviour modelling may include how to initiate conversation, how to take turns, how to share and how to care for other people.

There are often important distinctions between the contributions of the nurture group teacher and the TA. Whilst teachers will tend to take the major responsibility for planning the curriculum and assessing students' progress, the TA will share with the teacher the delivery of the curriculum. The precise ways in which teaching tasks are divided between teacher and TA will often depend on individual characteristics and/or preferences. For example, the teacher or TA may have a particular preference or flair for particular activities, such as reading aloud, art, cooking, computing or outdoor activities. In addition, there may be times when a student has a stronger affinity for one of the two adults than the other. In effective nurture groups, such preferences are exploited by the staff to maximise student engagement. A key quality shared by effective nurture group staff is that they do not take these kinds of issues personally.

It is not uncommon for TAs to come from the same local communities as the students attending the school (Roaf 2003). Whilst it is also the case that some teachers will also be from the local community, this is probably less common overall. In either case, knowledge of the local community that is gained from living within it can be very useful in helping staff to understand important issues affecting the lives of their students. An important principle here is that of flexibility among nurture group staff. The teacher/TA team works best when both share a common understanding of nurture group principles and practice, get on well together as people and support each other in utilising their personal strengths and aptitudes (Cooper and Tiknaz 2005).

4. The place of nurture groups within wider school life

Carers of children who attend nurture groups may express worries about their children being separated from their mainstream classrooms. These worries are often heard during the early stages of students' nurture group career. A classic nurture group is located within the physical boundaries of the school and is expected to fit in with the regular school timetable. The nurture group students are separated from their mainstream settings for certain periods of school time but they are still within and a part of the wider school system. In addition to registering every morning with their mainstream class and attending the class for at least half a day per week, nurture group students usually share lunch and break time with their mainstream peers so that they keep in touch with their peers and mainstream teachers. These measures help to ensure that attendance in the nurture group does not bear the stigma of exclusion (see carers', teachers' and students' perceptions in Chapters 3 and 4). In fact, nurture groups help these students to better adjust to mainstream classes by supporting their specific needs in ways that are not easily achieved in mainstream classrooms.

For some students, the nurture group is an alternative to being excluded from the mainstream school. Also, attendance in the nurture group is always seen as a temporary measure with full-time placement in a mainstream classroom as the most desirable eventual outcome. It follows that a useful way of thinking about nurture groups is as a form of transitional arrangement that is part of an inclusive educational environment.

5. The nurture group room

In setting up nurture group rooms, a deliberate attempt is made to create a comfortable and cosy environment that has the many features that one might expect to find in a traditional home. A classic nurture group room contains soft furnishings, kitchen and dining facilities (Boxall 2002). Also, nurture group rooms usually have a sofa and comfortable chairs around a carpeted area. This provides a space for group work and play. The kitchen allows the preparation of breakfast and cooking activities. As may be the case in a home situation, the dining table is used for sharing meals, as well as doing schoolwork. There could also be a number of other tables, just as would be found in any classroom.

This dual use of the dining table is much more than simply a practical use of available furniture. Imagine you are a student with very negative experience of classrooms. The very furniture of the classroom (the chairs, the desks, the whiteboard, etc.) may easily come to be associated with feelings of anxiety, apprehension and failure. It is for these reasons that some students develop highly negative reactions to the physical experience of being in a school or classroom. The dining table in the nurture group on the other hand, with its place mats, crockery, and associations with being fed and engaging in informal conversation in a relaxed atmosphere, carries with it highly positive connotations. The dining table is associated with pleasure and social acceptance. In fact, 'breakfast' is commonly the single most popular aspect of nurture group routine that is identified by the students. These positive feelings can help to counter the negativity that may be associated with formal classrooms. Thus, when a student is using the dining table as a workplace, the positive feelings that are associated with the table may help the student overcome some of the negative feelings associated with sitting at a school desk. We suggest that the symbolic meanings associated with the 'homely' features of the nurture group (e.g. soft furnishings, carpets, curtains) play an important role in helping students feel emotionally secure enough to engage with social and educational activities in the nurture group.

It is very important that we develop a sensitivity to the ways in which aspects of the physical environment can come to be associated with negative, sometimes destructive, emotions. The development of positive feelings and associations provides the bedrock for emotional growth and intellectual development. Healthy attachments between people reflect the development of an identification of feelings of being cared for and protected with a particular person. Similarly, the physical environment that is associated with those feelings has a very significant role to play. When students become attached to schooling, they are in effect acknowledging the association between schooling and feelings of security and emotional well-being. These feelings are the product of the kinds of relationships that have been fostered in the educational setting. That this educational setting (i.e. the nurture group) provides respite from negative associations relating to the physical experience of the standard classroom can make a significant contribution to building a new set of positive associations.

Other features of the nurture group room can also be understood in terms of this need to create an educational experience that is rooted in feelings of emotional security. Therefore, as in any mainstream classroom, there will be at least one computer which students will use to learn the basics of information and communication technology skills, as well as working on computerised tasks such as educational games. On the other hand, unusual for a standard classroom, most nurture groups will contain a full-length mirror. Again, the function of this everyday household item can be quite complex. Obviously, students will tend to take opportunities to study their reflections. This can be a very important part of the developmental process. When a student begins to take notice of how they look, they are beginning to develop a sense of how they might appear to other people. This process of standing outside of oneself is the beginning of the development of empathy. Empathy is concerned with looking at the world (including ourselves) through the eyes of other people. This ability is extremely important to human beings in enabling them to understand and regulate the effect of their behaviour on other people. It is not uncommon to see students in nurture groups 'pulling faces' at the mirror and in so doing experimenting with the effects of different facial gestures.

More recently, some nurture group staff and pupils have used digital cameras to capture images which represent certain special occasions and desired behaviour outcomes. For example, staff can take images of pupils working hard, enjoying celebrating a birthday together, or a co-operative play activity. These images can be hung on the walls for pupils as demonstrations of desirable behaviour and of the joy of being in a nurture group.

6. Play opportunities in nurture groups

Another special characteristic of nurture groups is the opportunities available for playing as a part of daily nurture group routine. Play in nurture groups has specific purposes. Play could be an individual or a shared activity. When it is an individual activity, the student might personalise the toys and use them to express his or her feelings (Boxall 2002). Toys could also be used by nurture group staff to develop the feeling of care for others (*ibid.*). Through play of this kind, students can experiment with different forms of social engagement. At first this may take the form of solitary play in which the student adopts different personas. It can then develop into social play in which several students adopt different roles.

Nurture groups should have a wide variety of play materials available. They will generally include sand and water, soft toys, jigsaws and a variety of other toys. In addition, nurture groups should have a range of materials to support role-play activities, including 'a dressing up box', and role-play scenarios such as shop and restaurant sets.

Play is in itself a form of exploration and experimentation to which the student brings his or her cognitive, social and emotional resources to bear. When students engage in play they are identifying and solving problems as they encounter the unexpected situations to which their free-flowing imaginations are taking them (Broadhead and English 1994; Moyles 1989; Slade 1995; Wood and Attfield 2005). Observing students at play can reveal very important clues about their stage of emotional and social development. The free playtime in nurture groups allows this kind of observation. For example, it is important to distinguish between students able to play in a solitary manner in a constructive way from those students whose play appears to be aimless. Also, the extent to which students are able to engage in productive co-operative play can be distinguished from those who appear to have difficulty playing with others. These differences are likely to be indicative of different developmental needs and will help nurture group staff determine appropriate targets and support for individual students. One of the key indicators for students' readiness for full-time integration into the mainstream classroom will be the demonstrable ability and willingness to engage in constructive co-operative play with other students.

When play is a shared activity, students have a chance to learn about the rules of social engagement and develop and improve their social communication skills (Bodrova and Leong 1998; Oden and Hall 1998). Through play, students learn and practise how to approach others; how to negotiate access into games that others are already playing; and how to invite others to join them in play. Social play is also a situation in which students learn the importance of following, creating and obeying rules. Therefore play makes a vital contribution to the development of real-life skills that students need in order to function socially. The kinds of co-operative relationships that emerge out of constructive play activities are essential prerequisites for the development of effective communication and learning.

Imaginative engagement is a very important aspect of play. This involves the mention of a situation, setting or an event which the individual engages in an exploratory and sometimes experimental moment (Nourot 1998). By learning how to deal with the unexpected, imaginative play provides a mental rehearsal for children for their social development by offering a forum for experimentation with new roles, situations and solutions (Coplan and Rubin 1998); it may also contribute to their language development (Williamson and Silvern 1984). Nurture group staff often exploit play opportunities which appear to emerge from the learning task.

Overall, play has a very important role in developing students' thinking and social communication skills. If play sessions are structured effectively, it has the potential to help students to connect the school experience with their inner world. Moreover, play is enjoyable for both children and adults, and so contributes to the positive emotional climate that characterises the successful nurture group.

THE NURTURE GROUP CURRICULUM

A curriculum sets out what students should learn and how they should be helped to learn. In this way it provides guidance for teachers on what to expect in terms of what students at a particular stage of development are likely to know, understand and do in a given area. In the UK teachers are expected to plan their teaching and carry out assessment on the basis of national guidelines (the exact nature of these guidelines differs between England and Wales, and Scotland and Northern Ireland). Obviously, in other countries where interest has been shown in nurture groups (e.g. Canada, New Zealand and the US) account will have to be taken of local national curriculum arrangements.

It can be argued that traditional approaches to the curriculum are narrowly defined and generally focus on defining what students are capable of doing by the end of certain stages in their school life in cognitive terms. The term 'cognitive' is very broad, and can be used to refer to a variety of features of the learning process such as perception, attention, information processing, memory, reasoning, problem solving and organisation of thinking. In simple terms, cognition is concerned with the mechanics of thinking. However, it is now widely acknowledged that, although important, these elements of human learning do not represent a comprehensive account of this area. What is missing from this formulation is an appropriate emphasis on social and emotional dimensions. It is fair to state that curriculum designers are becoming increasingly aware of this issue, but reform is slow moving and there is still a strong emphasis on cognitive over social and emotional dimensions.

Current primary and secondary school curricula in the UK have a strong cognitive focus in that they frame the specific knowledge and skills that students are expected to master at different stages of their school experience. Students are expected to understand new concepts by linking them with what they already know.

Whilst thinking and information processing skills are very important in students' development, there is far more to learning than just these skills. There is a growing body of research evidence which suggests that learning strongly affects and is affected by emotions and feelings. Published evidence suggests that different emotions and their intensity affect cognition differently. For example, when a student is depressed this will often have an impact on their ability to pay attention and access memories. It has been found that depressed individuals tend to allocate less of their resources to a given task because they tend to be distracted by negative thoughts (Ellis and Ashbrook 1988). Depressed students tend to show a lack of effort and enthusiasm for learning and socialising. For these reasons depressed students often engage in learning tasks less efficiently than students who are not depressed.

Anxious students often exhibit a range of attention problems, such as narrow attention span, and they appear to be more easily distracted. Anxiety is often associated with worry, which has a negative effect on information processing, motivation and memory (Eysenck and Calvo 1992; Eysenck and Keane 1995).

The Nurture Group Curriculum is strongly influenced by an understanding of the relationship between emotion, behaviour and social activity. However, this does not mean that thinking skills are not important for the Nurture Group Curriculum. The key point of this holistic approach to curriculum is that it recognises the ways in which emotional, behavioural and social barriers can prevent learning from taking place. A major aim of the Nurture Group Curriculum is to remove such barriers, to use positive emotion as a means of enhancing students' learning experiences.

In keeping with the main underpinnings of a classic nurture group, the Nurture Group Curriculum aims to provide students with the opportunity to access a broad-based balanced curriculum (NGN 2001). This curriculum was produced in 1997/1998 by the staff of Enfield nurture groups and has been used widely since then (NGN 2001). The curriculum provides a structure to guide teachers on the nature of student learning and direct attention to specific areas of student development that the nurture group is best placed to address. The Nurture Group Curriculum encompasses the National Curriculum (in England) alongside specific aspects of social, emotional and behavioural development.

The Nurture Group Curriculum is divided into the following sections:

- personal, social and health education
- communication, language and literacy; mathematical development
- scientific knowledge and understanding
- humanities and creative processes.

1. Personal, social and health education

The section on personal, social and health education (PSHE) is a vital part of the Nurture Group Curriculum and is derived directly from the nurturing philosophy (NGN 2001). This strand of the curriculum aims to provide early learning experiences for students and concerns with students' application of basic knowledge and simple skills (such as using toilets independently, using knives and forks and helping put things away with and without supervision). A crucial aim of the PSHE is to support students' positive social, emotional and behavioural development, as outlined in Table 2.2 (NGN 2001).

As we can see from Table 2.2, the Nurture Group Curriculum aims to promote positive, constructive social skill development. These skills include: selecting from a repertoire of possible behaviours, a response to the behaviour of another person; being able accurately to judge and interpret the behaviour of other students and adults; being aware of the likely consequences of their behaviour and making behavioural choices based on this; and listening to others constructively and assessing social situations.

Some of these items may, at first glance, appear to be trivial. This, however, is not the case. The more advanced social and thinking skills always depend on more elementary skills. Therefore, where elementary skills are absent, it is impossible to develop the more advanced skills. For example, the advanced skill of being able to read a social situation or understand how another person might be feeling on the basis of observing their behaviour cannot be developed until the individual has basic attention skills and a vocabulary for describing what they see.

It follows then that the kind of basic skills referred to in Table 2.2 are crucial for students' adjustment to school and their development as independent

Table 2.2: The outline of personal, social and health education in the Nurture Group Curriculum

Co-operation with others	• Plays co-operatively with adults.
	• Can play alongside one or more children with some interaction.
Sharing	• Can share books and toys with supervision.
	• Can share books and toys without supervision.
Expressing feelings	• Can understand basic words describing feelings.
	• Can express how they feel using words.
Initiation	• Asks for help from adult when appropriate.
Appropriate in-class behaviour	• Sits quietly in small group.
	• Sits quietly in large group.
	• Greets others appropriately.
	• Can play outside with other children without interfering.
Coping with unexpected	• Can cope with a change in routine.

Based on NGN 2001

individuals. Problems with these very basic skills usually indicate the need for the student to be given direct coaching in the missing skills. Without such coaching, students are likely to find the school experience harder than their peers and to be at greater risk of exclusion and of being bullied.

The fact that some students require further support in the areas outlined above should not necessarily be interpreted as a failure on the parents' part. For some students it may take longer to gain these skills than for others. One of the main purposes of the Nurture Group Curriculum is to identify gaps in students' repertoires of social skills and fill these gaps.

2. Communication, language and literacy

Improving students' communication skills and their literacy is a vital aspect of the Nurture Group Curriculum. Communication problems constitute one of the major reasons for nurture group placements. Difficulties in communication have adverse effects on students' abilities to initiate, construct and sustain interactions with their peers and adults.

The Nurture Group Curriculum outlines four different sections to recognise and address the issues related to communication, language and literacy. These are speaking, reading, listening, and writing and spelling. Table 2.3 highlights a number of selected aspects of what nurture group students are expected to achieve in these identified areas.

As illustrated in Table 2.3, nurture group students are expected to progress in their reading, writing, speaking and listening skills. There is also a gradual process in terms of how nurture group staff support these skills. For instance, in the first stages of their experience, the nurture group staff can only ask questions requiring simple answers, such as 'what does this do?' and 'what is this for?' (Boxall 2002). Throughout the later stages, students are encouraged and expected to provide explanations and to make comments, and to be able to deal with more complex questions.

The language used by the nurture group staff and the nature of communication between the teacher and the teaching assistant is explicitly used to exemplify the rules of communication; they tell personal stories, they show interest in and listen to each other (Boxall 2002). The students are also encouraged to listen and talk coherently with the nurture group staff and their peers.

3. Mathematical development and scientific knowledge and understanding

The mathematical and science development in the Nurture Group Curriculum is developed from 'Curriculum guidance for the foundation stage' and the mathematics and science of Key Stage 1 National Curriculum (Boxall 2002). Mathematical development in the Nurture Group Curriculum is mainly concerned with the identification of numbers, counting and making simple calculations. It also addresses the concepts of measurement, such as time, length and weight, money and volume. Specific attention is devoted to the recognition of shapes and the concept of space.

The curriculum on scientific knowledge and understanding is concerned with the development of basic physical, chemical and biological concepts. These are: life processes and living things; humans as organisms; materials and their properties; and some key physical processes such as electricity, force, light and sound (NGN 2001). Through exploration of these concepts, nurture groups enhance students' knowledge and understanding of important everyday concepts, thus enabling students to make better sense of the world around them, as well as preparing them for more complex scientific studies.

4. Humanities and creative processes

The Nurture Group Curriculum specifies what pupils should be able to achieve in humanities and their creative development. The creative component of the nurture group curriculum specifies the ways in which pupils could demonstrate

Table 2.3: The outline of the Nurture Group Curriculum's requirements in relation to communication, language and literacy

Speaking	Reading	Listening	Writing and spelling
• Use body language and facial gesture to communicate needs.	• Look at pictures in books with adults.	• React to sounds within the room.	• Play with writing material.
• Speak to familiar and unfamiliar children and adults.	• Look through books at random.	• React to sounds outside the room.	• Have some control over pencil.
• Ask and answer simple questions.	• Recognise that pictures tell stories.	• Look up when name is heard next to speaker and across the room.	• Place letters randomly on the page.
• Take turns at speaking and listening in conversation.	• Retell favourite stories.	• Recognise nursery rhymes or songs.	• Write strings of letters.
• Take part in a sustained conversation with an adult and peers.	• Show an awareness that text relates to pictures and has meanings.	• Recognise familiar objects by their sounds.	• Make marks from left to right.
• Initiate conversations with known and unknown adults and peers.	• Recognise characters/objects from pictures.	• Join in with actions for familiar songs or rhymes.	• Write independently, valuing own work.
• Talk about current and past activity with appropriate order of occurrences.	• Appreciate emotions in stories and responds.	• Anticipate routine events from sounds.	• Write own name.
• Use tenses correctly.	• Recognise that a group of letters make a word.	• Identify matching sounds.	• Write the initial letters of some words.
• Listen to a story and comment appropriately.	• Match one word to a picture.	• Clap rhythm of own name.	• Understand that words are groups of letters.
• Listen to simple and complex questions and make appropriate verbal response.	• Locate starting point and direction for reading print.	• Follow simple two stage instructions.	• Write underneath words that child has dictated.
	• Show awareness of some initial sounds.	• Follow simple three stage instructions.	• Leave spaces between words.
	• Guess a word from the first letter and words that look similar.	• Listen to a story in a one-to-one situation.	• Use sound/symbol correspondence.
	• Know sounds of some words.	• Listen to a story in a small group for two to three minutes.	• Know some simple spelling.
	• Have sight vocabulary of high interest words.	• Listen to a story in a small group for five minutes.	• Use upper and lower cases.
			• Write several sentences.
			• Use capital letters and full stops.
			• Know that spelling follows rules.
			• Use a variety of sources for spelling.

Based on NGN 2001

creativity through painting, modelling, music and a variety of materials. An important aim is to maximise pupils' opportunities to demonstrate their imagination and express their feelings and ideas in creative ways. The humanities element specifies the key components of geographical awareness, such as being able to identify different places and people in photographs and make comparisons between home and school. It also aims to develop pupils' historical knowledge and skills by developing pupils' understanding that events have causes and effects as well as encourage pupils to use time-related vocabulary such as 'when', 'after' and 'before'. The aim of this component is to develop pupils' basic knowledge, understanding and skills in history and geography and to prepare them for further learning in the mainstream classrooms.

At first glance the Nurture Group Curriculum appears not to be very demanding. Indeed, this is purposive and the original Nurture Group Curriculum was created with the learning needs of one to three-year-olds in mind. It should be realised that students of all ages can experience problems with some of the kinds of learning that are outlined in the Nurture Group Curriculum. Where this is the case, the older the child the more problematic such difficulties may be. On the other hand, of course, there will be students in nurture groups who are already proficient in many of these skills and functions. In effective nurture groups, staff differentiate their teaching in accordance with their assessment of individual students' specific needs. In other words, they calibrate their support on the basis of their assessment of students' prior knowledge and understanding. This means that not all students in nurture groups follow the whole curriculum as outlined above, rather they access the curriculum in accordance with their specific needs.

A TYPICAL DAY IN A NURTURE GROUP

The previous sections covered the thinking behind nurture groups and their curriculum. Now it is important to illustrate how this thinking is translated into practical activity in the nurture group. The following covers a typical classic nurture group day.

1. Registration with the mainstream class and transfer to the nurture group classroom

Nurture group students are registered with their mainstream teachers and are collected by the nurture group teacher or the teaching assistant. Once in the nurture group room, a typical day might begin with nurture group staff and students sitting in a circle and engaging in apparently informal conversation. Before engaging in the day's activities, students could be invited to share any news or comments that they wish. They are also encouraged to talk about their feelings, such as how they feel that particular morning. These types of activities are consistent with the personal, social and health education dimension of the Nurture Group Curriculum which promotes sharing between children, co-operation with others and the expression of feelings.

Such morning activities have been found to be a useful way of preparing students to engage with learning and co-operation. The nurture group teacher and the teaching assistant facilitate this activity by making sure that students listen to each other, value each other's emotions and take turns to speak. This activity helps students to improve their communication, and prepares them for engagement in the coming day.

This type of start of day activity can easily be carried out in a mainstream classroom. One would expect to see this type of activity going on in all of the classrooms of a nurturing school.

2. The first activity

Quite often nurture group teachers mention the agenda for the day in detail and make sure that students have an opportunity to know what to expect. Sometimes, the daily lesson plan is written on the board. This clarity of routine is important for helping students to develop feelings of safety and security. Uncertainty about what is going to happen in the future is likely to be a source of stress for anyone. This may be particularly the case for students in nurture groups whose prior experience of schooling has been distressing.

Nurture group staff pay special attention to the introduction of activities, and explain step by step instructions that students are required to follow in order to complete the learning tasks. This type of scaffolding appears to be intense in the early stages of students' experiences of nurture groups. Throughout the later stages, the nurture group staff may gradually decrease the level of control in the introduction of a task and try to develop students' capability to deal with the task without so much assistance, with the ultimate goal being for students to be able to work independently.

Nurture group classrooms follow a full curriculum with mornings being generally devoted to literacy and numeracy, and afternoons to science and foundation subjects. The nature of the activity can be varied depending on the curriculum topic and what the nurture group staff set out to achieve that particular day.

3. Breakfast

Breakfast is a very special part of a nurture group day. It is, on the one hand, an opportunity to learn and practise important social and communication skills, whilst on the other hand being a time for sharing and celebration. There are various stages in what might be termed the breakfast ritual. First, there is the preparation of the dining table during which one or more designated students wipe down the table and lay out place mats, cutlery and food items (sometimes this involves the setting out of name plates). Second, there is the preparation of the food (usually toast), and drink. At this stage, students and adults are consulted about preferences. Third, students and staff assemble around the table and food and drink is distributed. Fourth, the meal is consumed. Fifth, there is the tidying and washing up phase. Throughout the breakfast process there is constant verbal interaction (Cooper and Tiknaz 2004).

During breakfast, students have opportunities to talk to each other and exchange their ideas. Nurture group staff often promote conversations between students. The staff may also assist students with the application of basic skills such as the rules of eating and using cutlery. Sharing food during breakfast assists the creation and development of attachment and helps to promote a caring and loving atmosphere (NGN 2001). On some occasions, students and staff from other classes, or visitors from outside the school, are invited to share breakfast (e.g. parents, siblings of students and best friends). This is seen as a rewarding experience by nurture group students and their guests. In some cases, the invitation is itself a reward for a specific achievement or act by the visitor. Not surprisingly, breakfast is regarded very positively by students and staff (Cooper and Tiknaz 2004).

4. Returning to the mainstream classrooms for assembly

In some schools, after breakfast is finished, the nurture group students return to their classroom for assembly (NGN 2001). They may go alone, with other students or with a member of staff (*ibid.*). Assembly times may vary from one school to another but the reasoning is always the same. By returning to their mainstream setting, students' membership of the mainstream class is reinforced (*ibid.*). This also helps to prevent other students perceiving nurture group students as a separate cohort within school (*ibid.*).

5. Playtime

Nurture group students go from assembly to the playground with their mainstream class friends (NGN 2001). This is again an opportunity for nurture group students to meet with their mainstream peers outside the classroom context and could also help the nurture group students to maintain links with the mainstream classroom. Students in the playground are monitored by supervisors and if any of the nurture group students experience any difficulties the supervisors will intervene and if necessary seek the support of nurture group staff. It is, of course, important that playground supervisors are fully briefed as to the nature and function of the nurture group as part of the whole school policy.

6. The second session in the morning

After playtime, the nurture group students return to their mainstream classes to be collected by a member of the nurture group staff or go to the nurture group room independently. The second session in the morning may follow on from the first session or could address a different curriculum area. There are also usually play opportunities towards the end of the session in which nurture group pupils engage with their peers and with adults.

7. Lunchtime

It is common for nurture group students to participate in the regular lunchtime arrangements in the dining hall. However, it is not unusual for there to be special lunches held in the nurture group to which students from mainstream classes and other adults in the school can be invited. These may take place on a weekly, monthly or occasional basis. Such special lunches are often seen as celebratory (e.g. when a student has a birthday).

A significant proportion of the lunchtime period is devoted to free play. At the end of lunchtime, students attending the nurture group will usually return to their mainstream classrooms.

8. Afternoon session (in nurture group or mainstream classrooms)

After lunch the nurture group students are once again collected from their mainstream classrooms by nurture group staff. On some occasions, their mainstream teachers invite them to stay and participate in a regular class activity. This would include occasions when the whole class engage in some kind of fieldwork activity, for example visiting a museum or other community facility.

On some afternoons, designated nurture group students are given the opportunity to invite a friend from their mainstream classroom to join the nurture group for the first part of the afternoon. This helps to extend the nurture group experience to mainstream students and to increase their familiarity of what is happening in the nurture group (NGN 2001). This is also an important way of rewarding students in the nurture group and raising their status in the eyes of mainstream students. Of course, this is also intended to be seen as a reward by the mainstream students who are selected.

It is common for the afternoon session to begin with a whole group session, for example in the form of circle time. This is a brief period for communication and preparation for the afternoon session. The nature and implementation of the afternoon activity can vary and depends on the plan of the nurture group staff. However, very often the afternoon sessions are devoted to an art/craft activity which aims to develop the creative skills that are outlined in the relevant curriculum section. In classic nurture groups, each student is expected to engage in a reading activity during the afternoon sessions (NGN 2001). This can be individual, paired or shared reading depending on students' particular needs.

The individual student's participation in the afternoon session will often be dictated by the progress they have made since being in the nurture group. For many students, the closer they are to returning on a full-time basis to their mainstream class, the more flexible their afternoons will become, with an increasing proportion of the afternoons (or parts of afternoons) being spent in the mainstream classroom. The key concept here is that of flexibility. The close monitoring that students in nurture groups are subjected to enables finely calibrated decisions to be made about their specific needs.

It is very important, however, that any deviation from the normal routine of the nurture group be clearly justified to the student. The student's own preferences should always be taken into account. Also, the decision to have the student attend the mainstream class should be shared by nurture group and mainstream staff. These decisions may be made at fairly short notice, especially towards the end of a student's placement in the nurture group. The student's success in accommodating a change in routine at relatively short notice may well be a sign of the student's growing sense of emotional security. Obviously, in the early stages of a student's time in the nurture group, such changes in routine should be planned well ahead of time and the student be fully prepared for the change.

9. Afternoon break

It is increasingly rare for primary and infant schools in England to have a formal afternoon break time. This is regrettable. For many students, this means there is an unbroken period of two hours between lunchtime and home time. This comes at a point in the day when students are often tired and restless. Some nurture group staff compensate for this problem by giving the students a short period of semi-structured physical activity about halfway through the afternoon. This may involve the entire group going into the playground and making use of apparatus (which is likely to be unused at this time of the day) or engaging in more limited physical activity within the school building (e.g. 'brain gym' activities). At the end of this period, students are able to return to more sedate classroom activities, their restlessness having been dealt with.

10. Review at the end of the day

During the last session of the day it is useful if possible to review the day in a circle time session. In this part, nurture group students are encouraged to recall the key events of the day that they have just spent in school. The aim of this is to help students to go home with some sense of the positive achievements that they have made during the course of the day. This does not preclude reflection on things that may have gone wrong. On the contrary, being able to identify difficulties that have been experienced and highlighting lessons for the future that flow from these problems are very important learning experiences which contribute a great deal to personal and social development. The crucial point is that the nurture group day should end on as positive a note as possible for all students. Ideally, this will take the form of highlighting individual achievements and the awarding of, for example, tokens and/or points for positive achievements.

Over time, students are expected to become more proactive in identifying their own and others' positive achievements during the day. In the early stages, however, the nurture group staff will often take the lead in modelling ways in which positive behaviour can be identified and acknowledged.

SUMMARY

In this chapter, we explored the key characteristics of the classic nurture group. These are:

- The learning environment in nurture groups is predictable and carefully paced so that students feel safe and confident to engage in learning; have full access to staff support; and experience genuine success in meeting learning targets.

- The small size of the group allows the nurture group staff to communicate with students frequently and intensively. There are resources (e.g. more time, two adults working) for regular feedback and target setting on students' strengths and weaknesses in their learning and behaviour.

- The nurture group teacher and teaching assistant have special roles in supporting students. They constantly role-model for students and exemplify how to initiate and sustain positive communication with others.

- The nurture group room is designed in a comfortable way and items in nurture groups serve specific functions (e.g. mirrors for the development of an awareness of self as an independent, autonomous being; computers for developing information and communication skills; tables for sharing breakfast and work).

Students in nurture groups follow the Nurture Group Curriculum alongside the formal National Curriculum. The Nurture Group Curriculum acknowledges the interdependent relationship between emotion–behaviour–social skills and learning and outlines the expected progress in each of these areas.

CHAPTER 3

What School Staff Say About Nurture Groups

It is important to remember that when a student is placed in a nurture group he or she now has two teachers, one in the mainstream class and one in the nurture group, plus a teaching assistant (based in the nurture group), all of whom have a full-time interest in his or her education and well-being. All three of these adults have an important role to play in making sure that the student's social and academic needs are met. Also, from the parents' point of view, the availability of the nurture group staff, in addition to the mainstream teacher, means that there are more sources of information about their child's progress.

When teachers who have experience of working in or working with a nurture group talk about nurture groups they tend to say many of the same things that parents and students say. They see the nurture group as making a really important contribution to their ability to meet the needs of *all* students. In fact, when we think about what nurture groups can achieve for individual students, we must always remember that a nurture group can only work effectively for the students who attend it if the whole school is behind the nurture group. This means that an effective nurture group is part of a whole school set-up, in which all staff are working co-operatively with each other. After all, the main objective of the nurture group is to enable its students to return to mainstream classes on a full-time basis. If this is going to be achieved as much depends on what goes on in the mainstream classroom as it does on what goes on in the nurture group.

In this chapter we will explore the views of school staff about nurture groups. The information for this chapter comes from unpublished evaluation studies from more than 70 schools which have nurture groups in different parts of the UK, including Scotland. These evaluation studies were held by the Nurture Group Network. We also used our own research on nurture groups over the years.

MAINSTREAM TEACHERS' VIEWS

Mainstream teachers often have the experience of seeing students in their classrooms before and after they start attending nurture groups, and are in a strong position to comment on visible effects of nurture groups on their students. Such teachers often comment on the positive changes they see in students, often after as little as one term in the group. Typical comments include the observation of improvements in students' behaviour, their levels of self-confidence and their ability to form relationships with peers. From the teacher's point of view, a really important effect of the nurture group is that it often enables the student to be more engaged in what is going on in both the nurture group classroom and the mainstream classroom:

> Children are generally more willing to participate and are more responsive. (Mainstream teacher)

> Children come back [to the mainstream classroom] and seem to settle easily. (Mainstream teacher)

> The child seems more confident, wants to talk more and ask questions, which is positive. (Mainstream teacher)

Teachers also note that nurture groups tend to be most effective for students who display particular needs:

> Children who need emotional support, who get upset over little things; who get aggressive; who refuse to do things. Children who have emotional [difficulties and problem] behaviours who could do with additional support. (Mainstream teacher)

> Children who find it hard to cope with school life in the classroom environment. Children who need more of a special focus in a small group, not just learning but social issues and skills. (Mainstream teacher)

> I think it's a really good idea. Really nice. Children who do have difficulty in concentrating and find academic work difficult do get more support, and they've got a really nice environment to do it in. Children have five mornings and two afternoons in the nurture group where they do literacy and numeracy. Children can get much more support in the smaller group. They join the mainstream class in the afternoon for science, topic work and more arty things. They seem much happier. (Mainstream teacher)

As we can see in the above examples, students' needs vary in their nature and level. It could be that a child just needs a bit more emotional support to cope better in the mainstream classroom, or he or she just needs a bit more intensive support for numeracy or literacy. The above words confirm our starting point that nurture groups are for this extra support, and they are not for simply child-minding children who are excluded from their mainstream classrooms.

There is also an important practical spin-off for the mainstream teacher and other students in the mainstream classroom:

> The nurture group has alleviated some of the problems in the classroom environment that would have been there without the nurture group. (Mainstream teacher)

Another teacher expands on this:

> I think all of the teachers who have children in nurture groups would say teaching in their own class becomes a lot easier because you don't have to worry about those who [are in the] small special needs group in your class which could be quite disruptive and they are after constant attention. So to remove those children from the classroom in the morning when you do...literacy or numeracy hours [has] been a big benefit for all of us who have got children in there. It also means that the learning support assistant can also focus on sort of the middle group of children rather than having to keep their special needs children under control all the time... Personally speaking, my sort of next group made huge progress this year, and I don't think they would have done if those boys [attending the nurture group] had been in my classroom, because I had to put a lot of my support, time and energy to looking after those boys. The nurture group has been a great benefit. (Mainstream teacher)

This teacher is describing the way in which the removal of nurture group students created the opportunity to focus resources and energy onto a group of students who had been overshadowed by the perceived greater demands imposed by the nurture group students. This quotation suggests that the concentration in the mainstream classroom of a significant number of students exhibiting difficulties created a crisis situation in which the teacher felt unable to meet all students' needs effectively. The temporary placement of some students in the nurture group enabled the teacher to focus on the needs of this second group of students, whilst the nurture group students were being catered for in the nurture group:

> Having a child in the nurture group has alleviated the pressure of finding support for the child in the mainstream classroom. It enables you to deliver the curriculum and support other children's learning. (Mainstream teacher)

In the long run this led to a situation where, once the nurture group students were reintegrated into the mainstream, the teacher was in a better position to deal with the wide range of needs in her class.

It is important to stress that the mainstream teacher does not surrender responsibility for the students who go into the nurture group. On the contrary, where nurture groups are working effectively great emphasis is placed on the need for the mainstream teacher to be in constant communication with the nurture group staff, so that their own work with the nurture group students is enhanced by their knowledge of students' progress in the nurture group:

> I make sure that nurture group children are still part of the class and focus on that. I'm conscious that students attend two classes, and I manage the communications. In the nurture group they do different sort of work. The teacher has the long term plan so she can see what the rest of the class are doing. When the nurture group children come back to the classroom I work with them, if I feel they are able to do the work. There's a communications bag that is shared between nurture group teachers. It's to keep track, and to share anything nice that children have done. The emphasis is on the social skills, numeracy and literacy. It's different work from the mainstream classroom.
>
> The fact that the nurture group teachers come into the classroom is a big support to me – the dialogue and communication. And the Communication Folders that travel between the nurture group and the mainstream classroom. We can look at behaviour patterns over certain days to see if some days are worse or better, and to see if children were on task. It's a really good idea. (Mainstream teacher)

Having reviewed the mainstream teachers' views, what becomes clear is the importance of communication and co-operation between mainstream and nurture group staff to maximise and sustain the positive effects of nurture groups and protect its inclusive principles. We will now explore this issue in detail in the following section.

CO-OPERATIVE WORKING AND AVOIDING STIGMA

One of the things that some carers and school staff worry about, when they first hear about nurture groups, is the possibility that children who attend the nurture group will become stigmatised and be rejected by the children who do not attend the group. When there is good co-operation between the mainstream and the nurture group staff, such rejection does not occur. An example of one of the measures commonly adopted (to prevent stigma being attached to nurture group membership), in successfully functioning nurture group schools, is to create opportunities for all students in mainstream classes to get experience of being taught in the nurture group room. This is achieved through the mainstream and the nurture group staff working together to plan access to the nurture group room. On some occasions, students from the mainstream classrooms are invited to join the nurture group to play or to have breakfast with nurture group students. At other times, small groups from the mainstream classrooms are able to use the nurture group room when the nurture group students are not using it. Also, the nurture group staff can spend time in the mainstream class, working with all children. These simple measures add value to the work that goes on in the nurture group:

> The rest of the children have responded really well. They don't say to nurture group children 'you go out to that classroom'. They like to go and visit. They've all been to see the classroom and they like it. They're very accepting. [The nurture group] hasn't affected the relationship that children have with each other. A nurture group child is making closer friends with other children in the class, gaining skills that are more social. Wanting to work on the same table as them, whereas before he wanted to work on his own. (Mainstream teacher)

> It's been nice to have something new. Children from other classes have visited the nurture group. It's been good to look forward to, and good to do. It can only be a positive experience for the children in the nurture group. Working in a small group, rather in the classroom. In the classroom some children can become stressed. It's too big and too much and some children can lose control. The nurture group is a nice provision and people like it. Children like going and enjoy it. Sometimes they will tell you what they've done. (Mainstream teacher)

> It's very helpful when the nurture group staff come around in the after-noons. The children can see that we talk to each other, even when they're not in our classrooms. The children in the classrooms feel part of the nurture group because the nurture group teacher has spoken to them all, showed them around and had lessons, like they would have in their own classroom with the big books. The nurture group teacher reads them a story. She was very good with it. They could see it was the same as being in our classroom. I think the idea was that every class in the school went to visit the nurture group to start with, and then we would see after that. It would be nice if they had a chance to go again because they really enjoyed it. (Mainstream teacher)

It would be wrong to create the impression that things always run smoothly in nurture groups. In the early stages of being in a nurture group, some children can find the experience of transferring from one classroom to another quite difficult to deal with. However, these problems can often be overcome through the patience of mainstream and nurture group staff and co-operation between them:

> The changeover is very difficult between the two classrooms. Very difficult. A child has thrown chairs and hasn't wanted [to do] what the other children were doing. Now the child's more comfortable. [He is] enjoying the classroom and wanting to participate. The child also has a better relationship with the nurture group and me, and sees that as a staff we talk to one another. When a child's had a bad morning in the nurture group or the classroom, the child knows that each teacher will know about it. There's good communication. We've both got good relationships with this child. The child responds better to us than he does anyone else. I send his work over to the nurture group teacher so they can see. (Mainstream teacher)

This illustrates the way in which effective staff in schools work together in order to create a positive experience for the student. At the heart of this work is the effort to build *caring and supportive relationships* between staff and students.

CREATING A NURTURING SCHOOL

In different parts of this book we often make references to the impact of nurture groups on the overall school. The research evidence repeatedly reinforces this point. Mainstream teachers commonly describe the ways in which having a nurture group affects their thinking and practice. They believe that the presence of the nurture group, and interaction with nurture group staff, lead to insights being shared about different ways of understanding and approaching students exhibiting difficult behaviour and problems of adjustment. Two of the mainstream teachers described this influence as follows:

> Having the nurture group in the school has made us aware of what we do here and made us think about children more. We have started to think about emotional literacy... [In all classes] we all try to spend a bit of time chatting to children during the day as teachers, but we are hoping to take this a bit more on board as well... So, we are going to have toast and bread and something to drink (milk) in the morning. It is a nice start to the day. We will also invite parents to join in [and enjoy]...a bit more quality time with the children, which the nurture group inspired. (Mainstream teacher)

> I think what they do in the nurture group is nice. [It makes us think] 'why don't we become a little bit nurturing in our mainstream classes?' (Mainstream teacher)

Consideration of children's emotional needs is something that the NG made me think about more. This encouraged me to listen to children more. (Mainstream teacher)

NURTURE GROUP STAFF'S VIEWS

When nurture group staff talk about nurture groups they are often able to talk in detail about individual students. In particular, they are able to identify small, essential steps in students' progress which have to be taken to enable their participation in mainstream classrooms. Nurture group staff often note improvements in students' self-esteem and confidence; social skills; literacy and numeracy; and purposeful engagement in classroom learning. In the following, we will explore the nurture group staff's views in detail.

Improving students' in-class behaviour

By looking at a number of research reviews and evaluation studies, it becomes clear that nurture group staff are particularly concerned with improving students' in-class behaviour. Nurture group teachers agree that effective nurture groups help to improve students' behaviour in ways that enable the students to be effectively integrated into their mainstream classroom. Here, 'improvement' has different meanings for different students. For instance, one nurture group teacher describes the success of one student in terms of being able to 'learn how to sit sensibly' in carpet time; for another it is 'to manage to sit at the table more than 15 minutes to finish a worksheet'. Although at first these targets may appear trivial, it is important to realise that students' failure to be able to perform these behaviours can result in a barrier to effective participation in classroom life (in both nurture group and the mainstream classroom). A guiding principle for nurture group staff is that a student's failure to be able to carry out simple tasks is always a cue to teach the child the required behaviour, rather than to assume the student is being deliberately defiant.

From case studies of nurture group students, we can identify a number of success stories showing substantial behavioural improvements. The following anecdote represents only one of the many examples of such students:

> His behaviour became so extreme that his mother was asked to collect him at lunchtimes, he could attend school for half days only... He began in the nurture group room in September 2002. His Boxall Profile gave extreme scores away from the 'norm'. At first he found it difficult to participate constructively and accommodate others, he showed some inconsequential behaviour but never any violence towards other children or the staff. He quickly began to respond to the approach taken in the nurture group. He

was the first to learn the class rules and show affection toward the other children and staff. He would spontaneously hug others and got great pleasure from positive attention and praise. He soon wanted to please the teacher and the classroom assistant. If he made a bad choice at lunchtime or around school and got into trouble he would honestly explain what he had done and why. Temper tantrums became extremely rare as he began to realise he did not need to display this behaviour in order to be listened to. He began to share nicely with others, [and] could explain what was fair and unfair. A caring nature began to emerge and he'd be the first one there if someone fell or hurt themselves. (Nurture group teacher)

Nurture group staff are particularly concerned with promoting students' engagement in lessons. By engagement, we mean participation in what is happening in the classroom in a positive and constructive way, both intellectually and socially.

The ultimate sign of success is the return of students, on a full-time basis, to their mainstream classroom. One nurture group teacher summed up how this was achieved with one student:

She was overlooked because she could not present herself in the mainstream classroom, that is why she needed us, a place to find her own voice. So, that is what we did. We rebuilt her confidence and self-esteem back. Because of these factors she could not push herself forward in the classroom and academically she was underachieving, which is not the case any more. (Nurture group teacher)

This quotation highlights the importance of the intimate atmosphere of the nurture group and how this can help to meet the needs of students, who could easily be overlooked in a busy, over-sized mainstream classroom. In this case, a shy and withdrawn student is encouraged to develop a positive sense of self that translates into greater self-confidence that enables her to return to the mainstream classroom as a full participant who is now making good academic progress.

The importance of balance

Nurture groups are not designed solely for students who exhibit disruptive or challenging behaviour in the classroom. Whilst such students can be catered for in the nurture group, the membership of the group should not be composed entirely of such children. Experienced nurture group staff are very clear that the *balance* of students in the group is an important feature of well-functioning nurture groups:

We did think a lot about balance… We could have had ten children with challenging behaviour, but we did not view this as appropriate. We have a number of quiet children. One girl is mute and does not talk, [and there are] a number of children with emotional, social and educational difficulties. Without balance, it is hard to provide role-models. You can always say I am very pleased with so and so because they have done this or they have been sitting beautifully. If you don't have balance, it becomes difficult. (Nurture group teacher)

This draws attention to the importance of selection procedures. When considering a student for placement in a nurture group, staff need to consider not only the effects that the nurture group will have on that individual student, but also the effect that that student will have on other individuals in the group and the group as a whole. In the carefully controlled environment of a well-run nurture group, where the positive aspects of students' behaviour are searched for and highlighted, students who may have been seen as uncontrollably disruptive in the mainstream classroom can be encouraged to channel their liveliness and energy in more positive directions, thus providing positive role models for more withdrawn and introverted children. On the other hand, the positive attention and support that is directed at the quieter children provides the more extrovert students with new models of behaviour. As we have already noted, it can be very easy for the quiet student to be ignored in the mainstream classroom. This is not the case in the well-run nurture group.

Assessment of students' needs

The nurture group set-up offers enormous opportunities for assessing students' needs. The close observation of students is an integral part of the nurture group approach and this enables the development of detailed insights into students' needs:

Although the vast majority of children have made progress, there are two cases that haven't... Here [in the nurture group] we are dealing with children whose needs are enduring, extremely complex and in some ways we have to acknowledge that they may be beyond the scope of a nurture group. However, I don't consider this as a failure, I actually consider this as a success because this has given us the time and opportunity to gather the evidence to be able to pull in other agencies to provide support so that these children can also access the National Curriculum. (Nurture group teacher)

This means that even if the nurture group is not an appropriate placement for a student, the nurture group provides important opportunities that will help to identify students' needs and, therefore, help identify what interventions would be appropriate. Thus, it would be very rare for placement in the nurture group to be a waste of time.

Developing students' social and co-operative skills

Nurture group staff are often particularly pleased with improvements in students' social and co-operative skills. They often relate these improvements to the constant role-modelling provided by nurture group staff, and the increased opportunities available for students to interact with one another in well-structured small group situations. These improvements are observed within the nurture group setting and in mainstream classrooms, as well as in the home situation:

> I had one little boy who was very withdrawn, wouldn't talk at all, speech problems, just generally very shy and wasn't ready for school. He's now ready to come out of the nurture group after being there for a year, on and off, and he's chatty in the classroom, he'll talk to the children/teachers and if you walked in the classroom you wouldn't recognise him as a withdrawn child. (Nursery teacher)

> He is very chatty and willingly contributes to class discussion and activities. (Nurture group teacher)

> She is now in her third full term of being in the nurture group... Her speech and language have really improved. After a referral to [the] speech and language [service] she attended for two or three sessions before being discharged. Her speech is much clearer and she will often try to use adventurous vocabulary in her conversation. (Nurture group teacher)

Improvements in self-confidence and self-esteem

Nurture group staff often refer to improvements in students' self-esteem and confidence:

> Now, she can talk and answer my questions with a confident voice. You could hardly hear her voice two terms ago. (Nurture group teacher)

The increases in self-esteem and confidence were also reflected in improvements in students' self-images. This is shown in the way in which they talk about themselves as learners:

> His attitude to work has also improved greatly and he now has a more positive 'I can' approach to more formal school activities. This is in marked contrast to his previous 'I don't want to' response. (Nurture group teacher)

Taking responsibility for their own behaviour

Nurture group staff describe how students' behaviour improves as a result of their developing a sense of personal responsibility over their behaviour, and the way in which they encourage students to see their behaviour in terms of free choices that they make. An important part of this process is discussing with students the consequences of their behaviour and how different behaviour can lead to different (positive and negative) consequences. Nurture group students are reported to become more effective in developing a sense of control over their behaviour and, therefore, more able to comply with mainstream rules and routines:

> He still likes to have the teacher's attention to the exclusion of the other children (he will quite frequently want to sit on the teacher's knee and have a hug) and is very impulsive. However, he has become more aware of his feelings [towards] others and the effects of his behaviour on them. He is now much more willing to accept [the] restrictions and routines of the classroom. He conforms well to the rules of the classroom, accepting both rewards and sanctions, although he can still, at times, be very volatile. (Nurture group teacher)

> Slowly, she began to respond to praise and reward for positive behaviour with clear boundaries and parameters being set. During her first term in the group, she would display sullen moodiness when challenged or when a boundary was enforced, but gradually became more accepting and mature in her attitude. After two full terms she was willing to accept responsibility when she had done something wrong and would often be the first to say sorry and encourage other children to do so, in order to draw a line under an incident. This was something she would never have done six months earlier. (Nurture group teacher)

Increases in positive thinking and happiness

Nurture group staff suggest that the majority of students appear to be calmer and happier when they settle in nurture groups:

> She is now in her third full term of being in the nurture group. She has grown into a helpful, cheerful, polite child who will try her best to be positive. Her sense of humour has become more evident as episodes of sullenness have decreased. She will often amuse [us] with little dances or attempt to tell jokes. (Nurture group teacher)

Carers also commonly refer to the children's improved attitude towards school and improvements in levels of happiness. Students' own accounts further reinforce the view that the nurture group experience is a source of personal happiness (see above).

HEADTEACHERS' VIEWS

Headteachers play a very important role in contributing to the success of a nurture group. All of the headteachers whose views we have gathered appear to be supportive of the nurture group, and are very visible in declaring the support publicly to their colleagues, students, and the students' parents. A particular issue that headteachers commonly refer to is the significance of a nurture group within the context of the school as a whole. Many headteachers see the nurture group as either a means of rolling out a nurturing approach throughout the school, or they see the nurture group as a product of a whole school nurturing philosophy that was in existence before the nurture group was set up. Headteachers' positive response was very often driven by their own observations of improvements in students:

> The provision of a nurture group, I believe, has plugged a gap by providing for those children whose needs cannot be met by simply providing additional literacy and numeracy support and effective PSHE programmes. The nurture group is addressing children's insecurities; developing their self-esteem, and turning unhappy, withdrawn, uncooperative, disaffected children into happier, more confident, curious children who begin to see a place in the world for themselves and realise that education has something to offer them, and that they have lots to contribute to it. I have witnessed a transformation in particular children who I suspect would have created a problem throughout their educational careers but who are now happy to share their experiences and their learning with their peers and adults alike. (Headteacher)

Headteachers suggest that nurture groups affect schools in a number of crucial ways. In the following, we explore the nature of this impact.

The effect of the nurture group on the whole school

When headteachers were asked about their views on nurture groups, their immediate response appeared to be a recognition of the positive impact that nurture groups have on the whole school. Headteachers suggest that the acceptance and integration of nurture groups become easier when the school value system is compatible with the key nurture group principles:

> The nurture group fitted into what we had on offer already. We had opportunities to talk and to build relationships. We had lots of Circle Time and

emotional intelligence opportunities. Although the nurture group has had an impact on the school – my nurture group is in the school because of the things we had in the school. (Headteacher)

For one headteacher, the nurture group approach was part of a general pattern of change already underway in his school:

I was acting head during the period when the nurture group was set up. At that time we were adopting a 'caring educational community' approach…we were moving to new ways of working – outside the traditional ways of working… We were looking into new initiatives to expand children's horizons and experiences in the school. The nurture group was seen as another one of those initiatives. It was at a very appropriate time… [The] nurture group has very nicely fitted into that whole philosophy and vision for the way that the school is going… We want to be a welcoming, nurturing and caring school. These are the words I would like to hear in this school. (Headteacher)

Nurture groups appear to function more effectively within schools where there is an emphasis on developing nurturing and caring relationships.

In some cases, the nurture groups themselves help to create such an atmosphere by encouraging schools to reframe their behavioural policies, as one of the headteachers suggests:

The nurture group has also had an impact on the whole school. We have looked at our rewards and sanctions policy in order to incorporate some of the basic philosophies of the nurture group into our everyday practice. (Headteacher)

This statement suggests that having a nurture group can help alter the ways in which all students in schools are managed. However, the effects are not only reflected in the management of children but also in the philosophy shared by the adults working in the school:

The nurture group initiative has become an essential part of the ways we support children in school. The ethos of caring for all of them no matter how difficult they are is something that I feel is very important and says a lot about the type of school we manage. I have had requests to admit children because parents have heard we are a 'nurturing school'. I am very proud of that. (Headteacher)

It has an inestimable contribution to the raising of standards here… The nurture group has demonstrated that change can be effected in the most problematic children by patience and perseverance. There is no doubt that nurturing is infectious and that a whole culture and climate in a school can be altered. (Headteacher)

It becomes clear that these headteachers believe that effectively functioning nurture groups help schools by providing them with a framework for supporting students, in particular the ones who are at risk of exclusion. This is not only about what is being done to students within nurture groups, but also about the changes in school staff approaches towards and behaviour management of all students. Such impacts suggest that nurture groups can help schools to become more inclusive.

Underlying what many of these headteachers are saying is the realisation that 'nurturing' is not something that can take place in a vacuum. It would be inappropriate for a school to have a nurturing approach for some students whilst adopting a punitive approach to other students. Staff soon come to realise that if the nurturing approach has such a positive effect on a relatively small group of students who are having serious problems adjusting to mainstream classroom life, it is also likely to have the same effect on students whose behaviour is problematic but who in all other respects are relatively well adjusted to schooling.

The nurturing approach is also much more in keeping with modern, commonly accepted approaches to effective teaching in general than are punitive approaches to discipline. It has long been realised that students cannot be forced to learn anything and effective teaching is centrally concerned with facilitating constructive, willing engagement in a socially co-operative and emotionally supportive environment.

It is also clear that headteachers believe that nurture groups empower school staff to support students with challenging behaviour often in new ways. A key factor in this empowerment is the realisation, based on observing the progress of nurture group students, that persistence with and commitment to nurturing principles and practices often produces positive effects in improving the behaviour of students who may have been the subject of repeatedly unsuccessful attempts to modify their behaviour through sanctions and punishment. This experience of success is often associated with improvements not only in student self-esteem but in staff self-esteem as well.

The impact on relationships between school staff and carers

One of the main benefits of having a nurture group is the development of an open and inclusive culture not only within the school but also beyond the school. Headteachers often observe the development of stronger links between carers and the school community which they attribute to the nurturing approach.

Nurture groups can help to construct this positive relationship in a number of ways. Some headteachers describe nurture groups as providing a new access point for carers into the school. Carers who may have found themselves in difficult and sometimes strained relationships with school staff often find the nurture group staff easy to approach and welcoming. This is not intended to be read as a criticism of the way that some staff behave towards carers. However, it is the case that prior to placement in the nurture group many carers experience the contacts with schools as revolving around difficulties and concerns associated with the children's progress. This in itself often creates anxiety and can lead to difficulties in communication which are alleviated for many carers when they see the positive developments that take place after their child has been placed in the nurture group.

The quality of communication that takes place between the nurture group staff and carers is often characterised in terms of positive constructive dialogue. For instance, headteachers exemplified a number of situations where some parents who had previously avoided parents' evenings became regular visitors to the schools after their children attended nurture groups.

Headteachers also recognise that carers' acknowledgement of positive change in their children helped them to develop a positive home–school relationship:

> Parents have been more positive and involved in their children's develop-
> ment and this has raised the self-esteem of all concerned. During the recent
> Ofsted inspection, one parent made a point of registering her gratitude
> with the lead inspector for the way both she and her child had been uncon-
> ditionally helped and supported. She also expressed her delight at the
> huge change in behaviour and attitude of her child. (Headteacher)

Headteachers quite often elaborate on the changing perceptions of parents that are often associated with the developing working partnership between parents and school:

> The parents of these children [nurture group children] who before
> appeared anti-establishment are now willing to work in partnership with
> the school. School is no longer a place for confrontation and they are proud
> of and striving to support their children's development. (Headteacher)

Additionally, headteachers remark that having small numbers of students in nurture group classes helps to increase the frequency of parent meetings, which in turn helps to develop a more positive school–home relationship.

The invisible long-term impact of nurture groups

The majority of headteachers strongly believe in the nurture group as an intervention that has positive long-term effects:

> The Nurture Classroom has a tremendous impact on the lives of the children within the group. Although we have seen improvements within the children, the real impact will not be felt for a few years yet. The funding of the project is crucial. We, as a school, would not be able to fund the project ourselves. We need to ensure that the nurture group becomes an integral part of the school, allowing children who have poor social skills, through no fault of their own, to gain access to the curriculum. This will enable them to gain the necessary skills, academic and social, and qualifications to play an active part within society and become lifelong learners. (Headteacher)

At this stage, we can distinguish the short-term and long-term impact of nurture groups. The observable short-term impact of nurture groups is the engagement of students who are at risk with the education system by helping them to gain the skills that are needed to cope with the demands of schooling. An important indication of success in this regard is the decrease in temporary and permanent exclusion rates of schools which have properly functioning nurture groups and which have a caring and nurturing school ethos. This means that students at risk of exclusion are given positive choices and chances within their schools for re-engagement, rather than being formally excluded or referred to an off-site provision (e.g. student referral units or behaviour support centre). The long-term expected impact is the prevention of anti-social behaviour, depression and criminal acts which have detrimental social and economical impacts on the society that we live in.

SUMMARY

This chapter focused on exploring the perceptions and views of mainstream and nurture group staff and headteachers. They suggest a very positive perception of nurture groups.

- Mainstream teachers appear to be pleased with the quality of students' social, emotional and behavioural development. From the mainstream teachers' point of view, the largest improvements relate to students' behaviour, their levels of self-confidence and their ability to form relationships with peers. These teachers believe that nurture groups often enable students to be more engaged in the mainstream classroom. Furthermore, teachers are enabled, through the presence of nurture groups, to focus on other students whose needs were not being met when the nurture group students were present.

- Nurture group teachers witness very positive outcomes from nurture groups in meeting students' social, emotional and behavioural needs. Main changes noted by nurture group staff include improvements in students' self-images and levels of self-control, as well as improvements in their social ability to engage socially with other students. Nurture groups are also valued for the opportunities they create to work intensively with individual students and to learn in greater detail about their social, emotional and learning needs.

- Headteachers value nurture groups for having a nurturing impact on the overall school. This is reflected in an increasing emphasis on relationships and care for all students, regardless of the extent of their difficulties. Reduced rates of school exclusions and the strengthening of the links between home and school are also noticeable effects mentioned by the school heads.

CHAPTER 4

Carers, Children and Nurture Groups

> To be honest, if I had known what a group like this could achieve, I would have paid for the support myself. It has just made all the difference.
>
> (Carer of nurture group child)

This chapter looks at what carers and children with experience of nurture groups have to say about them. A strong theme in this book is the need for school staff and carers to work together in a mutually supportive manner that places the child's best interests at the heart of their combined efforts. This may not always be as easy to implement as it sounds. It is common for the kinds of problems that often precipitate the placement of a child in a nurture group to be accompanied by tensions between carers and school staff. These tensions sometimes take the form of mutual blaming. The carer blames the school for mishandling or not caring about the child, whilst the school blames the carer for being ineffectual, disengaged or negligent in their parenting of the child. Clearly, sometimes there is justification on one or both sides for these concerns. The key focus of this chapter, however, is that if school staff are to foster the kinds of professional relationships with carers that are conducive to the positive development of the child, it is essential that they avoid the tendency to blame carers for their apparent deficiencies. The child's interests are almost always best served by a pattern of co-operation and constructive communication between school staff and carers. This, in turn, will be supported by mutual respect and trust.

CARERS ARE NOT TO BLAME

> My child was chosen for the [nurture group] class because [the child] is quiet. My child wasn't talking, and not getting on with other children. The

teachers saw him as a behaviour problem but [the boy] said he just didn't understand what he should do. He couldn't read at all.

My child is chronically behind, finding everything that extra bit difficult, like forming letters and learning the alphabet. They recognised my child had special needs.

He was seeing a child psychologist and he wasn't progressing in his own class. He spent a lot of time out of the classroom... I'd previously seen the headteacher because I was very concerned about my child's behaviour and education.

...my child didn't want to come to school and didn't want to do any work.

These comments are from four carers of children who attend nurture groups. As it happens, these are all carers of children between the ages of five and seven. What they are saying, however, can often be heard from carers of students of all ages – from kindergarten to year 12. Approximately 20 out of every 100 school children are believed to experience serious problems in adjusting to school (Walker, Calvin and Ramsey 1995; Youngminds 1999). These problems are often a serious cause for concern among carers. They may be worried about their child's educational progress. They may be asking themselves: what is going to happen if he or she continues to fall behind other children in reading, writing and maths? How is he or she going to cope next year and the year after if the gap continues to widen? What is she or he going to be able to do when he or she leaves school if they haven't mastered the basics? How is she or he going to survive when he or she can't seem to make friends with other children?

Carers may be anxious because their child is withdrawn or vulnerable, or because he or she is a potential danger to other children. Carers may be angry. Angry at the school for making life so difficult for their child. Angry at the child for not trying harder. Angry at the unfairness of having a child with these problems (why me?). They may even have feelings of depression or guilt, and ask themselves: have I done something wrong as a carer? Have I failed my child in some way?

It is important to stress that this book is *not* about blaming carers for their children's difficulties in school. Anyone who has the privilege to be a carer knows that parenting can be a daunting and difficult job. Some people would argue that it is the most challenging task that any human being ever has to undertake. It can also, of course, be a great delight. In fact, there are few activities in life that are associated with such extremes of emotion: one minute we are filled with exhilaration, revelling in the joys of parenthood, the next minute anxious, despairing and/or angry. Sometimes we are simply exhausted by the whole business of being a carer and the demands it makes on us. The simple fact is that this mixture of challenges and conflicting emotions is the hallmark of most worthwhile human experiences.

The celebrated child psychiatrist Donald Winnicott argued that life is hard work for all of us, carers and children alike: 'Even the most kindly, understanding background of home-life cannot alter the fact that ordinary human development is hard' (Winnicott 1964, p.125). Winnicott went on to suggest that dealing with difficulties and struggle are key characteristics of human development that are reflected in the microcosm of the family:

> What is significant is the individual's experience of developing from an infant into a child and an adolescent, in a family that continues to exist, and that considers itself capable of coping with its own localized problems – the problems of the world in miniature. In miniature yes...but not smaller in regard to intensity of feelings and richness of experience. (Winnicott 1964, p.175)

Although in this book we are primarily concerned with problems which children experience in the early stages of their lives, it is important to acknowledge that these problems are not simply restricted to the child. They also, as we have already noted, impinge on the lives of carers, as well as on school staff. In the following sections, children and carers' perspectives on nurture groups and how they impacted on their lives are discussed.

WHAT CARERS SAY ABOUT NURTURE GROUPS

Although the majority of carers appear to welcome the idea that their child might be placed in a nurture group, it is also true that some carers are not very keen on the idea. Usually, by the time members of the school staff have reached the point where they are ready to suggest that carers should think about allowing their child to be placed in the nurture group, the carers have already become aware that things are not going well for their child in school.

Whilst many carers see the less pressurised and more gentle regime of the nurture group as a promising alternative to being in a mainstream classroom, others are worried that the nurture group is a place where 'naughty' or 'slow learning' students are placed because they are not wanted in mainstream classrooms. They worry that once placed in the nurture group their child will become even more unhappy in school, because he or she will be stigmatised and therefore rejected by other children.

These are understandable fears. If not explained fully, nurture groups can look very much like what used to be called 'sin bins' or 'remedial classes', in which children with difficulties, in the past, were sometimes placed. The worst examples of these kinds of settings were indeed excluding, stigmatising and achieved little more than keeping students out of mainstream classes. This lowers children's self-esteem. This is not the case with properly run nurture groups. Even carers who at first are worried about having their child placed in a nurture group usually find after a very short period of time that their child is thriving in the nurture group, and this tends to cause them to rethink their own views about nurture groups. As one such carer commented:

> I had reservations [about the nurture group] at first. I was worried about the label of problem children in the class. A few comments made in the play-ground [worried me], and it did concern me. Some of the children have behavioural difficulties, much more severe than my child's problem. However, my child has gained confidence in [the nurture group] class and settled in well. It's the first positive thing the school has done. It's given the children who would normally be left behind a chance to progress. (Parent of child in Key Stage 2)

Typical carer comments suggest that not only are students' educational perfor-mances improving, but this is underpinned by significant improvements in students' attitudes to schooling and their willingness to engage in learning processes. In turn, all of these appear to be associated with a greater sense of emotional well-being and confidence among the students.

Carers' perceptions identified five distinct changes in their children's attitude, behaviour, emotional well-being and social and academic engagement with schools:

1.   Students who have previously been unhappy with school and reluctant or unwilling to attend become keen and enthusiastic about school after being placed in a nurture group for a brief period of time:

> [The nurture group] class makes my child want to come to school. My child's self-esteem was down, and now it's a little bit up. He didn't used to write his name and now he can. He's really trying. (Parent of child in Key Stage 1)

> Some mornings it's been a fight to get him dressed. But now he's in [the nurture group] class in the mornings he enjoys going to school. I haven't had that much feedback or a report. (Parent of child in Key Stage 1)

2.   Students who have been withdrawn and shy often become more outgoing and more willing to interact with other children after being placed in a nurture group:

> Before starting in [the nurture group] class, my child was not participating in groups, or activities, [he was] very shy, almost mute. And now it's wow! My child is speaking out and it's like I've got a new child, it's a real reform. (Parent of child in Key Stage 1)

3.   Students who have a history of being aggressive and difficult to handle become calmer and easier to get along with after being placed in a nurture group:

> It used to be hard getting my child into the classroom and harder still for me to leave. If teachers tried to stop my child they [the child] would kick out, not intentionally, but the aggressive behaviour was there. (Parent of child in Key Stage 1)

4.   Improvements of the type mentioned above are often accompanied by improvements in academic performance (particularly in the crucial areas of literacy and numeracy):

> The teachers saw him as a behaviour problem but [the boy] said he just didn't understand what he should do. He couldn't read at all. [Since being in the nurture group] his maths is OK; his writing is OK. He is much more confident, and talks to us about school now. His behaviour seems better at school now and he is more settled at home. (Parent of child in Key Stage 2)

> I feel she has really come on. She is more confident now, and answers questions. She does her homework really well and just gets on with it. She has really improved since she went in the group. I can really see an improvement in maths, both with mental arithmetic and writing. (Parent of child in Key Stage 2)

> He was getting help in his previous school but seemed to be dragging behind. He wasn't enjoying the work. He didn't understand what the teacher was saying. (Parent of child in Key Stage 2)

5.   Students' improvements in school are often accompanied by
      improvements in relationships at home:

> He was behind in his reading and writing for year 2, and I was aware
> of that. And he wouldn't let me help him with his schoolwork at
> home. I think the school thinks he is making progress. He will read
> to me at home now, and he is getting more co-operative. (Parent of
> child in Key Stage 2)

> She now shares more with us about what she is doing [at school].
> (Parent of child in Key Stage 2)

Although carers tend to cite all round improvements in their children's school
performance, there is sometimes a difference between the way in which students
perform in the nurture group and how they perform in their mainstream classrooms. This difference is often most noticeable in the student's early stages of
being in the nurture group:

> I think the small group is brilliant. She finds being in the big class horren-
> dous. The group has helped her loads. (Parent of child in Key Stage 1)

It is important to note that not all students do as well as one would like in the
nurture group. A small minority of carers have reported that their children have
not made the progress that they hoped for:

> He has been in the group over a year now. He likes to go, but I think he
> hasn't got enough learning... I see his class teacher, but I don't see his
> nurture group teacher. I feel I don't know what goes on in the group. I need
> to understand what he is doing a bit more. (Parent of child in Key Stage 2)

It could be argued of course that the fact that the student 'likes to go' to the
nurture group is highly significant. As we will see in Chapter 6, social, emotional
and behavioural improvements often precede academic improvements. However,
this carer's concern about the lack of contact with the nurture group teacher
might be taken to suggest that the carer is not given sufficient information to
judge whether or not the student's progress is satisfactory.

A second carer was concerned that her child's defiant behaviour was not
improving:

> He needs to be in a smaller class – perhaps one to one... He has always been
> the same but it seems to be getting worse... He enjoys going to the group,
> but I am not sure whether it has helped or not. (Parent of child in Key Stage 1)

It would be unrealistic to expect any form of educational provision to be certain of succeeding with all students. Nurture groups, like any other form of educational provision, are constantly trying to improve the ways in which they operate. It is not always possible to know why some students do better than others in nurture groups. Sometimes differences in performance are due to differences in the nature of students' difficulties. Some students may require things that the nurture group is not able to offer, such as specialist therapeutic support or placement outside of a mainstream school. Similarly, there may be aspects of the nurture group or the nurture group's relationship with the school that require attention in order to better meet the needs of the individual student.

Overall, research evidence suggests that carers are satisfied with their children's placement in nurture groups. In the largest single study (see Chapter 6) of carers' views of nurture groups, 81 carers (spread across 27 nurture groups in different parts of England) were questioned about their level of satisfaction with nurture groups. Eighty carers said that they were either 'satisfied' or 'very satisfied' with their child's placement in the nurture group. Only one carer indicated dissatisfaction. This was based on their view that their child had not made any noticeable improvements in academic performance or behaviour. The other carers all indicated that, after two terms, their children were happier in school, better behaved (where poor behaviour had been an issue) and making better progress in their studies than had been the case before being placed in the nurture group. One carer summed up her feeling of satisfaction with the nurture group and the sense of relief that she and her child felt when she said:

We are really proud of him now. (Parent of child in Key Stage 2)

WHAT STUDENTS SAY ABOUT NURTURE GROUPS

Students are often very positive about their experience of being in a nurture group. Nurture group students tend to emphasise the following key features of the nurture group experience:

- the quality of interpersonal relationships in the nurure group and their fondness for the nurture group staff
- opportunities for fun activities and play
- the quietness and calmness of the nutrure group environment
- the frequency and quality of staff support.

The frequency and quality of adult support

Older and younger students comment on the quality of the relationships they have with the nurture group staff, often describing them as being approachable, kind and good humoured. Typical responses from students include:

> They are nice teachers here 'cause when I can't do things, they help me, they realise I can't do as speedy as others but I don't feel stupid. (Key Stage 2 student)

> I like teachers, they help you. They go into lessons with you. I like maths here. In the nurture suite, when you don't understand, they help you. (Key Stage 2 student)

A crucial feature of nurture group experience is the way in which it facilitates students' social and academic engagement:

> It's good. You get to choose. I like snack-time, specially when I help. I play with my friend, and my teachers help me. They talk to me. They're good. I've got stars. We do lots of work. (Key Stage 2 student)

> It helps me and I like it… You have to work hard. Miss makes you, even if you don't want to. But most kids try in here. If you have a question; if you want some help, you get it quickly. It's good… I like talking to my teachers; getting stars…they don't give you them for nothing. You have to say if you really deserve it. I like my work. I get lots of help if I can't see how to do it. (Key Stage 2 student)

> I like the working, it's good. You get more help. It's got two teachers helping you, and you get to go on the computer every lesson. (Key Stage 2 student)

Older students appreciated that the individual attention that they receive in the nurture group is often not available in the mainstream classroom. They also appear to be aware of other benefits of the small group setting:

> The teacher teaches here. They will show you what you need to do. I understand things better in nurture group than the other classrooms. Here, they make sure you understand, they explain. It is like one to one, when you're stuck, you put your hand up and they come and help you. In other classrooms they may help you, but mostly, you can't get any help. (Key Stage 3 student)

> I didn't like maths in the other classroom, because I couldn't think because everything was a bit odd. Now I do it nice and slowly in humanities. And I

can do it when I do slowly. They show us the work. They help us to catch up with subjects that we do in other classrooms. They help us a lot. (Key Stage 3 student)

Sometimes with older students, they contrast the quality of relationships in the nurture group with less positive experiences in other settings:

I don't like a lot of teachers here [in the school]. Some teachers tell you what to do all the time. 'Do this, do that, I just explained, I can't be simpler than this. What is wrong with you? How can't you learn this?' In the end, I quit. I didn't get any work with supplies [supply teachers] too. They are even worse. She explains once and decides I can't do it... Here, [the nurture suite], they help you and explain to you many times... They [the nurture suite staff] encourage your confidence, talking. If you talk, they are nice to you, they help you out. Even if you can't understand and can't do things, I don't feel bad, I feel successful here. They help me a lot. (Key Stage 3 student)

The above quotations were provided by a mixture of students, some of whom were very quiet and withdrawn and others highly disruptive. Because the members of staff were able to give such close attention to each student, they were able to identify students' learning difficulties at an individual level, and provide carefully targeted learning support. The staff were also able to help some students to deal with anger problems by providing them with coping strategies to improve:

Nurture group helped me with my anger problem. It helps me to cool it down. Before I came, I could lose my temper any time. I could just snap and punch people, things like I used to slam the classroom door in my previous school... In the NG, they taught me to how to cool down... I now go to a quiet corner, count till ten...it helps a lot. (Key Stage 3 student)

Other pupils describe improvements in their ability to engage socially with fellow students:

I used to be bullied a lot... I did not have any friends, now I get on well with people... (Key Stage 3 student)

Opportunities for fun activities and play
When young children (five to six years old) were interviewed, they commented positively on the availability of play activities and equipment.

Older students also clearly valued opportunities for activities such as cooking and playing. Cooking in groups appeared to be a very popular activity for the majority of students for the shared fun:

> I like making new things in the nurture suite… I think it is the best place in the school. (Key Stage 3 student)

> We play games, we have breakfast, it is nice here. (Key Stage 3 student)

> I actually look forward to going there. (Key Stage 3 student)

> We cook together… I made lots of friends here. (Key Stage 3 student)

The quietness and calmness of the nurture group environment

Students of all ages find the quietness and calmness of nurture groups highly beneficial in contrast to experience in other settings:

> The place [the nurture group] is different. In other classrooms, people talk when teacher talks. Here, some people still talk but it is rare. It is often in the other classroom. (Key Stage 3 student)

> In the other [mainstream] classroom, students are naughty and shout a lot. I can't concentrate and I can't understand anything. In the nurture suite, I can concentrate, it is very quiet. (Key Stage 3 student)

> In other classes, there are so many people. In here, there is not. In other classrooms, I often get headaches, they are very very noisy. (Key Stage 3 student)

The majority of students felt safe and comfortable in the nurture groups. This is referred to explicitly by some students:

> [It is] very positive here. They [the nurture group staff] support you through the work. They make you comfortable. They help you and can give you something easier to do if you are stuck. (Key Stage 3 student)

The word 'comfortable' implies a sense of safety and security.

Students also valued the organised nature of the nurture groups:

> Well, the other classrooms, they are not actually that nice and tidy. In other classrooms, I don't know, there are a lot of kids, you have lots of lessons, more than what you need…you can't do cooking and fun things. It is really fun in the nurture suite. (Key Stage 3 student)

Students' accounts suggest that nurture group staff's positive and supportive approach played a key role in creating feelings of safety.

The overwhelming impression that is given by students who attend nurture groups is that they enjoy the experience. They often speak with pride about the quality of the nurture group environment, with its comfortable furnishings and colourful decor, and they appreciate the opportunities provided for free play. For many students, it is in the nurture group that they make their first friendships with other students of the same age. These friendships are built on a foundation of positive self-esteem, which in turn derives from the effect of caring and feeling good about themselves as individuals.

In the nurture group, students have the time, space and activities available to enable them to learn about their own interests and to develop the skills necessary for mastering new challenges in a group situation. They are individually supported in the development of social and academic skills through the high quality, caring relationships that nurture group staff work hard to create with all children. They are also given many opportunities to learn about how and how not to behave in order to get along with other people. It is not surprising, therefore, that students' feelings towards the nurture group are often very positive. Where before schooling was associated with feelings of unhappiness and stress, now they commonly talk about the pleasure they derive from being in school.

SUMMARY

This chapter looked at nurture groups from the points of view of carers, and children. Carers whose children had experience with nurture groups suggested that:

- Students who have previously been unhappy with school and reluctant or unwilling to attend become keen and enthusiastic about school after being placed in a nurture group for a brief period of time.

- Students who have been withdrawn and shy often become more outgoing and more willing to interact with other children after being placed in a nurture group.

- Students who have a history of being aggressive and difficult to handle become calmer and easier to get along with after being placed in a nurture group.

- Students demonstrated improvements in academic performance (particularly in the crucial areas of literacy and numeracy).

- Students' improvements in school are often accompanied by improvements in relationships at home.

There is evidence to suggest that carers benefit directly from their children's engagement with nurture groups on emotional terms.

Nurture group students expressed many of the positive views about the nature and dynamics of the nurture groups. Their responses drew particular attention to the following features of nurture group routine which they valued:

- the quality of interpersonal relationships in the nurture group and their fondness for the nurture group staff
- opportunities for fun activities and play
- the quietness and calmness of the nurture group environment
- the frequency and quality of staff support.

ACKNOWLEDGEMENTS

Chapter 4 is based on evidence drawn from several research sources. These include the first national study of nurture groups in England and Wales, carried out by Paul Cooper, Ray Arnold and Eve Boyd (funded by the Nuffield Foundation and the Department for Education and Skills), as well as case studies that have been carried out by Professor Paul Cooper, Dr Yonca Tiknaz and Janie Butler at the Centre for Innovation in Raising Educational Achievement, University of Leicester School of Education. In addition, information is drawn from a range of case studies that have been carried out by members of the Nurture Group Network.

CHAPTER 5

Selection of Students for Nurture Groups

In previous chapters the reasons why students may need nurture groups were dis-cussed. In this chapter, we will focus our attention on *how* students are selected for nurture groups. To understand this, we will look at the possible decision-making processes within schools, as well as exploring specific tools that are used to assess students' suitability for nurture groups.

IDENTIFICATION AND SELECTION

In the majority of cases, headteachers, special educational needs co-ordinators (SENCOs), nurture group teachers, class teachers and carers are involved in the selection of students for nurture group placements. These key people share their observations and provide each other with valuable feedback which informs the rationale for placement decisions. School staff also use assessment tools such as the Boxall Profile and the Goodman Strengths and Difficulties Questionnaire (SDQ) to examine the suitability of students for nurture group placements.

A typical decision-making procedure for nurture group placement can involve communication between different agents (see Boxall 2002). As Table 5.1 illustrates, the assessment procedure involves communication between school staff, as well as the use of psychological assessment tools. Carers should also be asked to contribute to the initial discussions about potential nurture group placements. When carers receive a letter of invitation, they usually attend the school to discuss their children's potential placement in nurture groups. At this point the school staff should explain clearly what nurture groups are and why their child might benefit from a nurture group placement. During these discussions, carers also have an opportunity to clarify any issues of concern and express and exchange their ideas. They can also greatly help school staff by providing information on their children's home behaviour, the nature of their children's relationships with them and with peers. Carers are usually informed either through letters or personal communication about their children's placements in the nurture group.

Table 5.1: Brief referral procedure

Concerns expressed by parents, or members of staff, are followed up by the SENCO.

↓

The nurture group teacher and the SENCO observe potential nurture group students in their mainstream classrooms. At this point, they may use the SDQ or other assessment tools.

↓

In some cases, an educational psychologist may provide an individual assessment, but this is not always necessary.

↓

Carers are sent an informative invitation by the school to discuss the possibility of nurture group placement.

↓

A final recommendation for placement is made by the nurture group teacher, headteacher and SENCO, in consultation with the class teacher and the carers.

↓

The class teacher completes the Boxall Profile in discussion with the nurture group teacher. This gives an initial assessment of the nature and extent of children's early developmental needs. This may happen at any stage of the selection procedure.

↓

The class teacher and the headteacher meet the carers and seek carers' views about a possible placement in the nurture group.

Based on Boxall 2002

Some carers tend to resist and express concern about their children's separation from their mainstream classroom teacher and peers. They may feel uneasy about the idea of a nurture group for different reasons (e.g. their beliefs about effective education). When this is the case, it is often helpful for carers to be invited to the school again for further discussion. As we illustrated in Chapter 4, these worries appear to fade away quite quickly, and parents feel more positive about nurture groups when they observe their children's improvement in cognitive and behavioural terms, generally within a short time (e.g. one school term).

ASSESSMENT TOOLS COMMONLY USED FOR NURTURE GROUP PLACEMENT

THE BOXALL PROFILE

The Boxall Profile provides a structured framework for the observation of students' behavioural, social and cognitive engagement in classrooms (Bennathan and Boxall 1998). It was developed by the educational psychologist Marjorie Boxall, who was the originator of nurture groups. The profile provides a means of identifying and monitoring changes in students' social, emotional and behavioural needs to plan for effective intervention. The profile consists of two major parts: the Developmental Strands and the Diagnostic Profile. Each of these parts is in turn divided into a series of 'strands', each of which is broken down into a number of sub-strands. The sub-strands are, in turn, composed of descriptive items.

Developmental Strands

The Developmental Strands identify a set of skills, some of which can be interpreted as relevant to students' pre-school experiences. These skills are crucial if students are to engage constructively and positively with educational activities. The Developmental Strands consist of two main strands named 'organisation of experience' and 'internalisation of controls'. Table 5.2 illustrates in detail what teachers examine when they make judgments about students' developmental characteristics (Bennathan and Boxall 1998).

Organisation of experience

This category broadly aims to assess students' responsiveness and engagement with their surroundings (Bennathan and Boxall 1998). Additionally, it examines the extent to which students are organised, attentive and interested and able to relate themselves to adults and their peers.

The organisation of experience requires the teacher to observe a number of skills which are crucial for successful engagement with school learning (Bennathan and Boxall 1998). One starting point is to understand the student's capacity for paying attention and his or her responsiveness to the teacher. For instance, the teacher may observe whether the student appears to listen with interest to the teacher's explanations. The teacher monitors the student's listening

Table 5.2: Developmental Strands

Organisation of experience

Gives purposeful attention	Participates constructively	Connects up experiences	Shows insightful involvement	Engages cognitively with peers
Listens with interest when the teacher explains to the class.	Shows awareness of happenings in the natural world, is interested and curious and genuinely seeks explanations.	Of his/her own accord returns to and completes a satisfying activity that has been interrupted.	Appreciates a joke or is amused by an incongruous statement or situation.	Contributes actively to co-operative play with two or more students and shows some variations in the roles s/he takes.
Makes appropriate and purposeful use of materials/equipment/toys provided by the teacher without the need for continuing support.	Shows genuine interest in another student's activity or news; looks or listens and gains from the experience; does not intrude unduly, does not take over.	Recalls information of relevance to something s/he hears or reads about and makes a constructive link.	Makes constructive and reciprocal friendships which provide companionship.	Engages in conversation with another student.
Listens, attends and does what is required when the teacher addresses a simple request specifically to him/her.	Is reasonably well organised in assembling the materials s/he needs and in clearing away; *reminders only are needed.*	Communicates a simple train of thought with coherence, e.g. when telling or writing a story or describing an event.	Responds to stories about animals and people with appropriate feeling, appropriately identifies the characters as bad, good, funny etc.	
Is adequately competent and self-reliant in managing his/her basic personal needs.			Makes persistent observations about the relationship between two other people, appropriately attributes attitudes and motives to them.	
Takes part in a teacher centred group activity.			Shows curiosity and constructive interest; is secure enough to accept a change.	

Internalisation of controls

Emotionally secure	Biddable, accepts constraints	Accommodates others	Responds constructively to others
Takes appropriate care of something s/he has done; *investment of feeling in the achievement is implied, and self-esteem.*	Begins to clear up to close an enjoyable work or play activity with adequate warning; makes a general request to the group.	Makes and accepts normal physical contact with others, e.g. *when holding hands in a game.*	In freely developing activities involving other children, s/he constructively adopts to their ideas and suggestions.
Turns to his/her teacher for help, reassurance or acknowledgement, in the expectation that support will be forthcoming; *disregards occasional normal negativism.*	Complies with specific verbal prohibitions on his/her personal use of classroom equipment.	Maintains acceptable behaviour and functions adequately when the routine of the day is disturbed, e.g. *when there are visitors in the class, or the class is taken by another teacher.*	Shows genuine concern and thoughtfulness for other people; is sympathetic and offers help.
Looks up and makes eye contact when the teacher is nearby and addresses him/her by name, i.e. *heads the teacher, does not necessarily pay attention.*	Works or plays alongside a child who is independently occupied, without interfering or causing disturbance.	Makes an appropriate verbal request to another child who is in his/her way or has something s/he needs; *disregards situations of provocation.*	
	Sits reasonably still without talking or causing disturbance when the teacher makes general requests to all children for their attention.	Accommodates to other children when they show friendly and constructive interest in joining his/her play or game.	
		Gives way to another child's legitimate need for classroom equipment s/he is using by sharing it with him/her or taking turns; *no more reminder is needed.*	

Based on Bennathan and Boxall 1998

and responding skills when he or she is asked a question or he or she provides an explanation.

Here, what the teacher observes has cognitive, social and behavioural dimensions. From a cognitive point of view, the teacher evaluates whether the student understands what is required from her or him and whether the student pays purposive attention to the situation. From a social and behavioural point of view, the teacher observes whether the student is able to participate constructively in social interaction and interprets the social situation in an appropriate way. This means the teacher looks for evidence of the extent to which the student is aware of the social rules necessary for working with others in a positive way (e.g. taking turns when talking in a social situation; being able to listen to others and making appropriate comments).

A further aspect of organisation of experience relates to the student's capacity for connecting new knowledge, understanding and skills linked to existing ones. This ability is indeed an important one and constitutes one of the underpinnings of Vygotsky's social constructivist theory, which is a major learning theory. For instance, when a story is read in the classroom, students' understanding and appreciation of the story depends on their ability to show appropriate feelings and be able to make links with their everyday life. Through the development of these skills students learn how to engage with and understand other people.

The student's interest in events, his or her ability to accommodate new experiences and their capacity to relate to adults and peers are all assessed through the Boxall Profile. A high score on this scale suggests that a student is well prepared to meet the social and cognitive challenges and demands of schooling.

Internalisation of controls

This strand assesses students' personal development and awareness of others (Bennathan and Boxall 1998). Overall, this section helps to determine whether or not students are emotionally secure; whether they are able to establish and sustain relationships with their peers; whether they can work effectively within group situations; and whether they have the internalised control that is necessary for their social functioning (*ibid.*).

The internalisation of controls strand provides a basis for assessing the student's personal development by looking at it from a number of angles. First of all, there are a number of items that measure the level of the student's emotional security by observing whether or not a student is 'self-accepting' and whether or not he or she displays a sense of self-worth and can trust others. Second, staff are required to consider items that describe the student's capability to accept organisational constraints, such as being able to leave an enjoyable activity to start a new activity or lesson. Furthermore, the internalisation of controls strand has items concerned with the student's ability to express his or her own needs, to accept others' needs, and his or her willingness and ability to co-operate with others effectively. Overall, these characteristics are important to the development of personal and social skills that are essential for effective functioning in social situations, and especially in the school setting.

Diagnostic Profile

The second major part of the Boxall Profile consists of items that identify potential barriers at the individual level of a student's functioning, and in relation to his or her engagement with others. This section of the profile has three strands. These are: self-limiting features; undeveloped behaviour; and unsupported development. Table 5.3 illustrates the characteristics of the Diagnostic Profile (Bennathan and Boxall 1998.

Self-limiting features indicate disengagement and the inability to relate to others. A student with self-limiting behaviour is more likely to appear to be insensitive to others. This may show itself in the student's lack of participation in social situations. By looking at the items set in the Diagnostic Profile, the school staff make judgements about the student's level of maturity, as revealed in his or her behaviour. The school staff are also looking for evidence of how the student perceives him or herself, as well as evidence of the absence of other skills necessary for relating to others and effectively engaging in learning. The school staff also assess age-appropriate behaviour in terms of the student's self-control and the way in which the student responds to social situations. These measures also allow the school staff to observe whether or not the student shows negativity towards self and others. High scores in this strand indicate an insecure, fragile self-image.

There is also a motivational dimension which refers to disengagement from an educational task or a play activity. For instance, the student starts the work but cannot sustain attention or motivation to complete it. The initial excitement (if there is any) tends to disappear very quickly. This could also be related to a very weak sense of purpose and not being able to sustain cognitive and motivational engagement without constant adult and/or peer support.

A further aspect of self-limiting features of behaviour relates to being insecure and extremely self-conscious ('self-negating' factors). A typical observation could be the student's difficulty in engaging in unfamiliar tasks or in challenging and competitive situations. The student may exhibit behaviour that appears to indicate that he or she is threatened. Relatedly, the student may appear to interpret any critical feedback as disapproval, and may internalise it in a destructive way. For instance, if the teacher criticises any aspect of the student's

Table 5.3: The Diagnostic Profile

Self-limiting features		Undeveloped behaviour		
Disengaged	*Self-negating*	*Makes un-differentiated attachments*	*Shows inconsequential behaviour*	*Craves attachment reassurance*
Oblivious of people and events; 'is out of contact and can't be reached'.	Avoids, rejects or becomes upset when faced with a new and unfamiliar task or a difficult or competitive situation.	Relates and responds to the adults as a baby would; enjoys baby-level pleasures; may happily babble and coo, call out or crawl about, or mirror the others.	Inappropriate noises or remarks, or patterns of behaviour that are bizarre fragments of no obvious relevance.	Adopts stratagems to gain and maintain close physical contact with the adult.
Repetitively pursues a limited work or play activity which does not progress.	Self-conscious and easily rebuffed, and hypersensitive to disapproval or the regard which s/he is held by others.	Over-reacts to affection, attention or praise; gets very excited and may become out of control.	Gives uninhibited expression to noisy and boisterous behaviour; is not influenced by normal social constraints and expectations.	Desperately craves affection, approval and reassurance, but doubts and questions the regard shown, seeks it repeatedly but remains insecure.
Listless and aimless; lacks motivation and functions only with direct and continuing support or pressure.	Self-disparaging and self-demeaning.	Clings tenaciously to inconsequential objects and resists having them taken away.	'Is into everything', shows fleeting interest but doesn't attend to anything for long. Restless and erratic, behaviour is without purposeful sequence, continuity and direction.	

Unsupported development

Avoids/rejects attachment	Has undeveloped/insecure sense of self	Shows negativism towards self	Shows negativism towards others	Wants, grabs, disregarding others
Abnormal eye contact and gaze.	Variable in mood; sometimes seeks and responds to affectionate contact with the adult, at other times rejects or avoids.	Uncontrolled and unpredictable emotional outbursts or eruptions that release and relieve pent up and endured anger and distress.	Erupts into temper, rage or violence when thwarted, frustrated, criticised or touched, the 'trigger' is immediate and specific.	Always has to be first, or have the most attention or get immediate attention.
Lacks trust in adults' intentions and is wary of what they might do; avoids contact and readily shows fear.	Contrary in behaviour; sometimes helpful, co-operative and compliant, at other times stubborn, obstinate and resistive, or unheeding.	Spoils, destroys, or otherwise negates the achievement or success s/he has worked for and values.	Reacts defensively even when there is no real threat, is evasive, blames others, finds excuses or denies.	Can't wait for his/her turn for something s/he wants; plunges and grabs.
Functions and relates to others minimally, and resists or erupts when attempts are made to engage him/her further.	Attention-seeking in a bid for recognition or admiration.	Sulks when disapproval is shown, or when attention is withdrawn, or when thwarted.	Disparaging attitudes towards other children; is critical and contemptuous.	
Sullen, resentful, and negative in general attitude and mood.	Can't tolerate even a slight imperfection in his/her work and is upset or angry if s/he can't put it right.	Feels persecuted; imagines others are against him/her, and complains of being 'got at' and left out.	Remembers a real or imagined offence, bears a grudge and determinedly takes his/her revenge.	
			Determinedly dominates or persecutes by bullying, intimidation, or the use of force.	

Based on Bennathan and Boxall 1998

work, he or she may interpret this criticism as an indication of his or her lack of ability rather than lack of effort or concentration. Self-negating behaviour is more likely to be associated with negative emotions about oneself and anxiety.

Undeveloped behaviour is characterised by immature responses and behaviour. Students with undeveloped behaviour will commonly be observed to exhibit the kind of behaviours most often associated with babies or very young children. For instance, the student may respond to teachers with baby-talk and may show baby-like pleasures.

Inappropriate social responses are another indication of undeveloped behaviour. Students showing undeveloped behaviour tend to have difficulty in understanding and interpreting social situations. These students may also be noisy and boisterous in their manners. They can be attention seeking and need constant approval and reassurances to function in social situations. Overall, undeveloped behaviour is often concerned with insecure emotional attachment, inappropriate responses and misinterpretations of social situations.

The unsupported development sub-strand section addresses students' capacity to form attachments with others, and the extent of their negativity towards themselves and others. Students exhibiting signs of unsupported development tend to present difficulties in forming attachments with adults and their peers. For instance, they may lack trust in others' intentions, avoid contact with others, and show fear of others' sustaining social interactions. Their engagement with others remains minimal (e.g. little or no eye contact).

An important feature of unsupported development is the student's 'negativity towards self'. Students exhibiting such behavioural characteristics tend to seek reassurance and approval constantly. When they perceive others as being critical towards them, or when others show disapproval, they tend to show behavioural signs of bad temper and annoyance. On some occasions, uncontrolled and unpredictable emotional eruptions can happen, in particular during stressful times. Negativity towards oneself, therefore, has a powerful impact on the student's ability to regulate their emotions, and affects negatively the ways in which he or she interprets others' responses and behaviours.

Unsupported development is also associated with negativity towards others. Students with these behavioural characteristics tend to be critical and disapproving of their peers and adults. On the other hand, they tend not to be self-critical, but defensive, and can blame others for their own shortcomings. Their social memory can also be selective, such as mainly remembering negative situations (even sometimes imagining such situations) to justify their own negativity towards others. In some cases, they may frequently exhibit coercive behaviour, and be involved in bullying others.

Having assessed the student on the basis of the criteria outlined in the Boxall Profile, the school staff may conclude that the student needs further support which cannot be provided fully in the mainstream classroom and the student may become a candidate for the nurture group.

THE GOODMAN STRENGTHS AND DIFFICULTIES QUESTIONNAIRE (SDQ)

The SDQ is a short questionnaire, which is widely used to assess positive and negative behavioural attributes of children and adolescents (Goodman 1997, 1999). There are different versions of the SDQ to be filled in by parents, teachers or students themselves (for 11 years and older). The instrument, therefore, provides an excellent opportunity to collate views of the student's behaviour from a variety of viewpoints, including the student's own perspective.

The SDQ generates information about:

- emotional symptoms
- conduct problems
- hyperactivity/inattention
- peer relationship problems
- prosocial behaviour.

For each category, the questionnaire provides five items. For each item, the person who completes the questionnaire chooses from three options ('not true', 'some-what true' and 'certainly true'). For each of the five categories (see list above), the student is given a score. There is also an overall score for the entirety of the test. Table 5.4 illustrates the nature of these attributes.

An additional feature of the SDQ is the 'impact supplement' (Goodman 1997). This is a short questionnaire on the reverse of the form that asks questions of a qualitative nature, in order to assess the degree of concern created by any difficulties that have been identified, which is felt by the respondent.

The SDQ is a recently standardised instrument. This enables the scores of the individual students to be compared with those of a much wider population. For example, it is normally assumed that 80 per cent of the students would score in the 'normal' range.

The SDQ is widely used for making nurture group placement decisions. Along with the Boxall Profile, it provides numerical information for monitoring students' progress on the five behavioural, social and emotional categories identified above.

Table 5.4: The items that appear in the Goodman SDQ

Emotional symptoms scale

- often complains of headaches, stomach aches or sickness
- many worries, often seems worried
- often unhappy, downhearted or tearful
- nervous or clingy in new situations, easily loses confidence
- many fears, easily scared

Conduct problems scale

- often has temper tantrums or hot tempers
- generally obedient, usually does what adults request
- often fights with other children or bullies them
- often lies or cheats
- steals from home, school or elsewhere

Hyperactivity scale

- restless, overactive, cannot stay still for long
- constantly fidgeting or squirming
- easily distracted, concentration wanders
- acts before thinking
- sees tasks through to the end, good attention span

Peer problems scale

- rather solitary, tends to play alone
- has at least one good friend
- generally liked by other children
- picked or bullied by other children
- gets on better with adults than with other children

Prosocial scale

- considerate of other people's feelings
- shares readily with other children
- helpful if someone is hurt, upset or feeling ill
- kind to younger children
- often volunteers to help others

Based on Goodman 1997

NURTURE GROUP PLACEMENT

Clearly, the numerical and qualitative information that is gathered through the use of the Boxall Profile and the SDQ is extremely useful in helping school staff come to a decision about whether or not a student should be placed in a nurture group. However, this data alone is not a sufficient basis on which to make the final decision. Even though the Boxall Profile draws heavily on the perceptions of the staff who know the student well, this data should always be used in conjunction with whatever additional information can be gathered revealing the judgement of experienced school staff who know the student and, of course, the knowledge and views of parents/carers and the students themselves. This means that formal and informal interviews can have a role to play in these processes.

In addition other sources of numerical data may be useful, including reading scores, measures of linguistic competence and self-esteem ratings. The final decision as to whether or not the student should be placed in the nurture group should be based on as wide a range of information as is available.

The assessment and decision-making processes illustrate the importance of collaboration and cooperation between key stakeholders.

SUMMARY

In this chapter, we explored how students are selected for nurture groups in schools. Very often, headteachers, special educational needs co-ordinators (SENCOs), nurture group teachers, class teachers and parents are involved in the selection of students for nurture group placements. These key people share their observations and provide each other with valuable feedback which inform the rationale for placement decisions. We also examined the assessment tools that are commonly used to assist the decisions regarding nurture group placements. We focused on two major tools: the Boxall Profile and the Goodman Strengths and Difficulties Questionnaire.

The Boxall Profile is a structured framework for observation of students' behavioural, social and cognitive engagement in classrooms (Bennathan and Boxall 1998). The profile provides a framework to identify students' social, emotional and behavioural needs to plan for effective intervention. The profile is also used for measuring students' progress throughout their experience in nurture groups. The profile consists of two strands: the Developmental Strands and the Diagnostic Profile.

The second tool is the Goodman Strengths and Difficulties Questionnaire (SDQ). The SDQ is a short questionnaire which is widely used to assess levels of positive and negative behavioural attributes of children and adolescents.

CHAPTER 6

Do Nurture Groups Work? Existing Research on Nurture Groups

Do nurture groups work? We have already shown in the first five chapters of this book that school staff, carers and the students themselves, more often than not, *think* that nurture groups work very well in bringing about positive changes in the ways in which students function in school. The evidence that we have presented so far has been drawn from two major sources: 1. interviews with staff, students and carers that were undertaken by a range of people who have worked as part of the Nurture Group Network, which include the authors of this book (Cooper and Tiknaz 2005), who have worked together with other colleagues (e.g. Cooper and Lovey 1999; Cooper, Arnold and Boyd 2000), as well as 2. nurture group practitioners and other LEA employees who have carried out small-scale evaluations of their own provision which they have shared with the Nurture Group Network (NGN). This is very important evidence in itself, but it is only part of the story.

We will achieve a much stronger picture of the effectiveness of nurture groups if we can gather evidence from a wider range of sources, including evaluation studies carried out by people who have worked independently of the Nurture Group Network and less subjective forms of evidence, by which we can test the validity of these subjective perceptions. By bringing this evidence together we will be able to decide if nurture groups are a worthwhile expenditure of effort, and if they are an efficient use of limited financial resources. These issues are very important to carers, school staff and students. They are also of particular interest to the holders of educational purse strings (i.e. national and local government, and individual schools).

In this chapter we review some of the existing research evidence on the effectiveness of nurture groups. Our review is based on original research published in scientifically respectable (i.e. peer-reviewed) journals, and books edited by respected academics in the field of education. We have reported on all of the recently published studies that were available to us at the time of writing. Therefore, this is not a selective review, but rather a snapshot of the available evidence as it stood in January 2007.

WHAT KINDS OF EFFECTS DO NURTURE GROUPS HAVE ON STUDENTS?

In one study, researchers assessed the performance of 68 five-year-old children placed in three nurture groups for a mean period of 3.1 terms (O'Connor and Colwell 2002). Using the Boxall Profile data, they found significant improvements in students' cognitive and emotional development, social engagement and behaviours. Other research studies also find similar results, which supports the view that nurture groups are effective placements for children with such needs.

Published small-scale case studies have explored the nature and effectiveness of nurture groups. One study of this kind, Bishop and Swain (2000a, 2000b), explored the effectiveness of a nurture group in an inner city area of severe deprivation with students between Years 1 to 3. In these studies, the school staff and parents expressed very positive views of the nurture group.

From the beginning of this book, we have referred to the importance of establishing and sustaining positive relationships between nurture group staff and parents. The nature of such communication has not been widely explored in the nurture group literature (Bishop and Swain 2000a is an exception). On the basis of a study of one school, these researchers suggest that the skills and expertise of teachers are passed on to parents through routine meetings when the parents visit the nurture group to pick up their children (Cunningham and Davis 1985; Dale 1996, cited in Bishop and Swain 2000a, p.22). The authors also make the crucial point that problems can be made worse if nurture group staff take a domineering rather than supportive approach to parents during this dialogue.

WHAT DO WE KNOW ABOUT WHAT HAPPENS TO STUDENTS AFTER THEY LEAVE NURTURE GROUPS?

An important early study was carried out by the Educational Psychology Service in the London Borough of Enfield (Iszatt and Wasilewska 1997) where nurture groups have thrived since the 1980s. This study found that, of 308 children who were placed in nurture groups between 1984 and 1988, 87 per cent were able to return to mainstream classes after spending less than one year in nurture groups. In 1995 this group was revisited, and it was found that 83 per cent of the original 308 were still in mainstream placements with only 4 per cent requiring Special

Educational Needs (SEN) support beyond the schools' standard range of provision. Thirteen per cent of the original group of 308 students were granted Statements of Special Educational Need, and 11 per cent of the 308 were referred to special school provision.

In this study, there was also a group of 20 mainstream students who had been designated as requiring nurture group placement but for whom places had not been found. A much higher level of persistent difficulties was found in this group, 35 per cent of whom were placed in special schools and only 55 per cent of whom were found, by 1995, to be coping in mainstream classrooms without additional support.

Iszatt and Wasilewska found that, in a typical nurture group of between 10 and 12 students, on average approximately ten students returned to the mainstream after less than a year, and received no further specialist support for the majority of their remaining time in full-time compulsory education. Students in this study who were not able to take up places in nurture groups were four times more likely to receive further SEN help than the students who were placed in nurture groups.

From a professional point of view, it could be argued that there is no reason to question the professionalism of staff in Enfield. On this basis, we cautiously conclude that the findings of this study are very promising. For such a large proportion of students who cause serious concern during Key Stage 1 to require no further support after being placed in a nurture group is impressive. Furthermore, this result is consistent with studies of staff perceptions of the effects of nurture group placement assessed in other studies, which point to widespread improvements in students' self-management behaviours; social skills; self-awareness and confidence; and skills for learning and approaches to learning (Boorn 2002; Cooper and Lovey 1999; Cooper and Tiknaz 2005; Doyle 2001; Lucas 1999).

THE FIRST NATIONAL STUDY (UK) OF THE EFFECTIVENESS OF NURTURE GROUPS

Up to this point, we have covered small-scale research evidence on nurture groups, mainly within one or a small number of schools. In exploring the nature and effectiveness of nurture groups, a major nationwide study was conducted (Cooper *et al.* 1998). In the initial stages of this study, the research team surveyed the existing nurture group practices in the UK. An important finding of this study was the identification of four different types of nurture group. In the following, we focus on each type in turn.

What are the major ways in which nurture groups differ from one another?

Type 1: The classic 'Boxall' nurture group

These groups show all characteristics of the model established by Marjorie Boxall (Bennathan and Boxall 2000; Boxall 2002). The 'Boxall' nurture group is a temporary and part-time placement (usually nine out of ten half-day sessions per week) for students with social, emotional, behavioural and learning difficulties. Consistent with the descriptions of the classic nurture group, there are two adults, a teacher and teaching assistant. The nurture group classroom consists of between 10 and 12 students.

One criterion in classifying the nurture groups is whether the nurture group students are selected from one school. In Type 1, students who attend the nurture group are only selected from the mainstream roll of the school in which the nurture group is located. It means that some nurture groups can have students from different schools, and the nurture classroom may be located out of school. However, this is not the case for the classic (Boxall) nurture group.

The classic nurture group follows the same patterns as we identified in Chapter 2 (registry with the mainstream class in the mornings, collection by the nurture group staff, free play time, daily 'breakfast', the use of the Nurture Group Curriculum). The identification of nurture group candidates and the monitoring of student progress are facilitated mainly through the use of the Boxall Profile and the Goldman Strengths and Difficulties Questionaaire (SDQ). As already mentioned, the main purpose of the classic nurture group placement is the return of nurture group students to mainstream classes on a full-time basis. In normal conditions, return to mainstream classes takes place after three or four school terms, though where appropriate this can take place after one or two terms.

Type 2: New nurture groups

Nurture groups of this type are based on the principles underpinning the classic model but differ in structure and/or organisational features from the classic nurture group on the basis of:

- the amount of time that students spend in these groups
- the composition of groups
- the location of groups.

The research found that these new types of groups do not follow the same routine which the classic nurture groups would follow. For instance, they appeared to run from half a day to four days per week in mainstream schools depending on the individual school's resources and arrangements.

Another key difference of the new nurture group relates to the composition and location of nurture groups. A nurture group of this type may serve a number of schools, rather than a single school. Therefore, the group may consist of students from a number of schools. The new type of nurture group can be located in a special school, or take the form of an off-site unit. The research also identified a 'travelling nurture group' covering a large geographical area and moved from one school to another.

Regardless of organisational differences, however, these groups employ core structural features of the classic nurture group approach, such as small group size, and being staffed by a teacher and a teaching assistant, and they adhere to the core principles of the classic approach by having a developmental emphasis and following the holistic Nurture Group Curriculum.

Type 3: Groups informed by nurture group principles

These are groups which sometimes keep the name 'nurture group', or are claimed to show similarities with the classic nurture group concept, but which often depart radically from the organisational principles of classic and new type of nurture groups. They may, for example, take place outside of the normal curricular structure of the schools where they are located. They can also run during lunchtime, break time or after school hours. Others may take the form of 'havens' or 'sanctuaries' that students join at different times. The groups may be run by a single individual or a non-teaching adult (such as a teaching assistant, mentor or counsellor). The activities that go on in these groups will tend to focus on social and developmental issues but do not have the academic emphasis of the classic and new variant groups.

Type 4: Aberrant nurture groups

These are groups which keep the name 'nurture groups' or are claimed to be types of the nurture group concept but, in fact, undermine or distort the key defining principles of the classic nurture group. These are groups that lack the educational and/or developmental emphasis which underpins the classic nurture group concept.

Comment on the variations

The first two types, the classic (Boxall) nurture groups (Type 1) and the new nurture groups (Type 2), might be seen as genuine nurture groups. The third type often provides important social and emotional support for students, though it is in danger of being peripheral. The fourth type is potentially dangerous, by promoting a distorted image of the accepted meaning and philosophy of nurture groups.

WHAT ARE THE EFFECTS OF NURTURE GROUPS?

The study by Cooper and Whitebread (2007) assessed the effectiveness of nurture groups in promoting positive, social, emotional and educational development. They studied the classic (Type 1) and the new (Type 2) nurture groups. Key issues explored were:

- the effects of nurture groups in promoting students' social, emotional, behavioural and educational improvement whilst they are attending the nurture groups
- the extent to which any improvements are generalised to mainstream settings
- the impact of nurture groups on whole schools
- the impact of nurture groups on parent–child relationships.

This study was designed to compare nurture group students with students who did not attend nurture groups. In the first group, there was a group of 359 students (71.5 per cent male; average age: six years five months) attending nurture groups. This group was compared with a second group, consisting of 187 students (matched to a random sample of nurture group students). The second group was made up of four different comparison groups, consisting of:

1.   sixty-four students with social, emotional and behavioural difficulties (SEBD) attending nurture group schools

2.   sixty-five students without SEBD attending nurture group schools

3.   thirty-one students with SEBD attending schools which did not have nurture group provision

4.   twenty-seven students who did not have SEBD attending schools that did not have nurture group provision.

Figure 6.1 shows the different groups.

In order to compare the different groups numerically, the Goodman SDQ and the Boxall Profile were used. Additionally, school staff, parents and students were interviewed. The researchers collected the numerical data each school term over two years.

Findings based on numerical data
What are the effects of nurture groups on students' social, emotional and educational functioning?

In order to evaluate the effectiveness of nurture groups, the researchers selected three groups. The first group consisted of all nurture group children (359

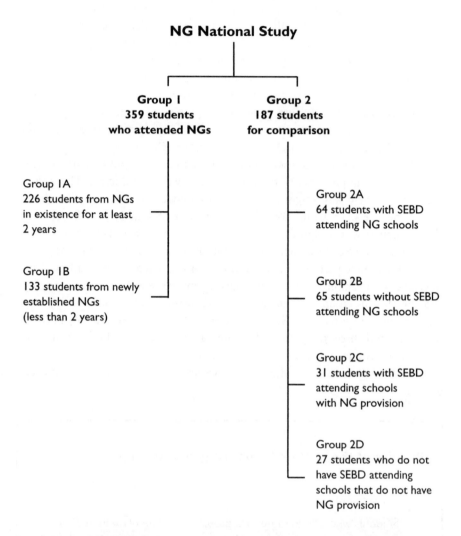

Figure 6.1: Comparison groups in the national study (Cooper and Whitebread 2007)

students, Group 1). The second group included students with SEBD in the schools which had nurture groups (64 students, Group 2A). Group 2A had similar difficulties to the nurture group students but did not attend the nurture groups, and remained in their mainstream classrooms in the nurture group schools. In the third group, there were students without SEBD attending nurture group schools (65 students, Group 2B).

The research reported very positive (i.e. statistically significant) results for the nurture group students. Overall, the nurture group students improved in their social, emotional and behavioural functioning (as observed by mainstream teachers when the students are in mainstream classrooms). The improvements were greater for the children in the nurture groups than the students with SEBD in the same schools who were not attending nurture groups (Group 2A and Group 2B). Although nurture group students started with generally poorer Goodman SDQ scores, they improved more quickly than the students in the same-school mainstream SEBD comparison group (Group 2A).

The researchers also used statistical measures to judge whether the differences in improvements between groups were significant. The results showed that there was a significant difference between nurture group students' scores and the mainstream controls who do not present SEBD (Group 2B). However, there was no significant difference between the scores of nurture group students and the SEBD students who are in the same school (Group 2A).

Measures taken termly (i.e. three times during a school year) allowed the researchers to examine the impact of time on improvements for the nurture group and comparison group students. It became clear that while behaviour improves for both nurture group and SEBD same-school controls (Group 2A) between terms one and three, the period of greatest improvement for both groups was between terms one and two.

The list below sums up the results measuring the effectiveness of nurture groups.

Results of the national nurture group survey

1. The nurture group students improved in their social, emotional and behavioural functioning.

2. Students who attended nurture groups and students with SEBD who were in the mainstream schools with nurture groups improved in their social, emotional and behavioural functioning to a far greater extent than students with SEBD that did not attend nurture groups.

3. When nurture groups were in existence for more than two years, their effectiveness was far greater than the groups which were in existence for less than two years.

4. Both the nurture group students and the comparison students with SEBD in the same school showed greatest improvements between terms one and two.

Comparing the progress of old versus new groups
The Goodman SDQ scores

The researchers were also interested in comparing the impact of old and new established groups on students' progress. They considered old groups as ones which had been in existence for more than two years prior to the start of the study. They compared old groups' progress with mainstream controls over the first two terms. The three groups involved were:

- Group 1A: Nurture group students (groups founded two years or more) (220 students)

- Group 2A: Mainstream students with SEBD attending the same mainstream schools (64 students)

- Group 2B: Mainstream students without SEBD attending the same mainstream schools (62 students).

Overall, the results suggest that old nurture groups were more effective in meeting students' social, emotional and behavioural needs than the newly established groups. The rate of improvement in the SDQ scores of the nurture group students (Group 1A) was significantly greater than the control students with SEBD (Group 2A). A detailed examination of the measures suggest that at the point of entry in the nurture group 91.8 per cent of the nurture group students were reported to be not within the 'normal range' as measured by the SDQ, as opposed to 84.4 per cent of the matched mainstream SEBD students. However, within a year this had reduced to 65.9 per cent for the nurture group students (a gain of just under 26 per cent), but only to 75 per cent for the mainstream comparison group (a gain of about 10 per cent).

The Boxall data scores for the nurture group students

As we noted at the beginning of this chapter, the national study used the Boxall Profiles in addition to the SDQ to evaluate the effectiveness of nurture groups. In the national study, the Boxall Profiles were completed only for the nurture group students.

The analysis of the Boxall Profile focused on measuring the rate of improvements for different periods of time. Measures were taken three repeated times over a period of approximately four school terms. The results indicated that nurture group students showed significant improvements between time 1 and 2. The improvements between times 1 and 3 was also significant on all Boxall scores. However, the differences between time 2 and 3 scores on the whole were less significant. This finding is consistent with the results of the Goodman data. This result suggests that it is more likely to observe students' improvements in their social, emotional and behavioural functioning between the first and second term of the placement in nurture groups.

An important additional finding here is that significant improvements on the 'organisation of experience' continue between times 2 and 3. This suggests that whilst improvements in social, emotional and behavioural difficulties tend to be most marked between times 1 and 2, improvements in behaviour associated with engagement with learning tasks continues, for nurture group students, over all three periods.

At the beginning of this chapter we reported the differences between nurture groups. An important aim of the national study was to explore how the differences between nurture groups affect their progress. In the following, we answer this question.

How do differences between nurture groups affect student progress?

The researchers identified a number of factors that have a likely influence on differences in performance between nurture groups. The findings to this question were generated largely on the basis of interviews with school staff, as well as the numerical data collected over two years. In the following, we explore the factors that have important impacts on the effectiveness of nurture groups.

Proportion of the school week spent in the nurture groups

An important factor affecting the success of nurture groups appears to be the amount of time students spend in the nurture group over the course of a week, with larger periods of time predicting higher levels of mean improvement. This applies throughout the period of placement. It is possible, however, that the longer established groups might be able to compensate for limited time through well-developed patterns of co-ordination between the nurture group and mainstream.

This research also highlighted the point that the nature of improvements due to the nurture group can be different depending on the amount of time that students spend in nurture groups. Students' social, emotional and behavioural functioning seems to improve greatly in the first two terms and there seems to be less significant and noticeable improvement after two terms. However, significant improvements in behaviours linked to students' engagement in educational tasks and activities continue into the third and fourth school terms. For students in nurture groups which have been established for two years or more, these improvements are of a statistically significant level, when compared to the improvements experienced by mainstream SEBD controls. This suggests that the effectiveness of nurture groups improves over time, as nurture group staff and the school as a whole become more familiar with working with the nurture group approach.

Balance in nurture groups

The nature of students' difficulties and the balance of groups also appear to be important factors for the effectiveness of nurture groups. Nurture groups appear to produce significant gains across a wide range of difficulties, in both SEBD and educational terms. When they are in the nurture groups, students presenting with internalising and acting-out patterns of behaviour show impressive rates of improvement. When they are in their mainstream classes, however, it is the students who have exhibited high levels of acting-out behaviours initially who seem to generalise their improved behaviour to the mainstream setting. Students who present with mainly social/emotional problems and exclusively hyperactive behaviour do not generalise the improvements made in the nurture group to the mainstream setting. This complex finding may be open to a number of different interpretations. One likely explanation is that the nurture group provides intensive social learning experiences that equip children who lack self-regulatory strategies with appropriate skills. On the other hand, students whose difficulties reside primarily at the level of unresolved emotional difficulties, or in the form of congenital problems with impulse control (e.g. as in the case of attention deficit hyperactivity disorder), will have these difficulties catered for in the nurture group (and hence will make positive progress there) but will continue to be vulnerable to ubiquitous features of mainstream classrooms (e.g. relatively higher levels of stimulation; lack of individual attention; more complex daily routine; greater emphasis on student self-regulation) which in turn stimulate their dysfunctional behaviour patterns. Of course, the more mainstream staff become aware of how to implement nurturing approaches the greater likelihood that children with these difficulties will be catered for. This is not to say, however, that there will not be some children who will require extra attention and respite from the pressures from the mainstream classroom through their attendance at nurture groups.

The stability of nurture groups

The national study suggested that whether or not the nurture group teacher had been replaced during the running of groups could actually have an impact on nurture group students' social, emotional and behavioural functioning. This suggests that stability of nurture groups is an important factor.

Nurture group students' fluency in English

Students' fluency in English appears to be a crucial factor in influencing the effectiveness of nurture groups. The importance of fluent English can perhaps be accounted for by the fact that nurture group practice is often characterised by intensive verbal communication between staff and students.

As we mentioned in Chapters 3 and 4, nurture group students' improvements in their social and communication skills were widely acknowledged by school staff and parents. The current findings suggest that nurture group students are in an advantageous situation to practise and improve their social and communication skills throughout their time in nurture groups.

Whole school effects of nurture groups

This detailed study found that nurture groups have added significantly to positive work that mainstream primary schools do with the students who have SEBD. An unexpected finding is that schools with nurture groups appear to work well with students who have SEBD who do not attend nurture groups. This was suggested on the basis that schools that have nurture groups achieve significantly higher gains for students with SEBD (both in the nurture group and in the mainstream) than the schools which do not have nurture groups.

In-depth interviews with school staff point to the contribution of nurture groups on the overall school staff in approaching and managing students with SEBD. The research interviews particularly indicated that when there is good communication between mainstream and nurture group staff, mainstream staff develop 'nurturing' approaches to use in their own classrooms. Thus schools that have well-functioning nurture groups appear to demonstrate nurturing approaches in their mainstream classrooms.

It is tempting to assume that these whole school effects are the result of having a nurture group in the school. That is, that the nurture group *causes* the whole school to adopt nurturing approaches. Whilst this may be the case, evidence from the perceptions of school staff, particularly headteachers, sometimes suggests that nurture groups are often adopted by schools which already profess a commitment to nurturing approaches (Cooper and Tiknaz 2005). In these cases, headteachers claimed that nurture groups enhanced rather than created opportunities for creating a nurturing environment in their schools.

Impact of nurture groups on carers

As we have noted in Chapter 4, carers often have very positive things to say about nurture groups. In this study 84 carers were asked whether or not they were satisfied with the nurture group attended by their children. Ninety-six per cent of these carers claimed to be either 'satisfied' or 'very satisfied' with their children's

nurture groups. When interviewed in depth, these carers reported that their satisfaction was related to what they saw as dramatic improvements in their children's
attitudes to school and social, emotional, behavioural and educational functioning. Some carers reported dramatic improvements in their own relationships with
their children that they attributed to the effects of improvements in their children's functioning in school.

SUMMARY

In this chapter, we reviewed research evidence to deepen understanding of the
nature and effectiveness of nurture groups. The national study review suggests
that:

- There are four types of practices that were relevant to the nurture group
  theme. The Type 1 nurture groups show all the characteristics of the
  model established by Marjorie Boxall (Bennathan and Boxall 2000;
  Boxall 2002) in terms of their philosophy and operations. Nurture
  groups of Type 2 are based on the principles underpinning the classic
  model but differ in structure and/or organisational features from the
  classic nurture group (e.g. the amount of time that students spend in these
  groups; the composition of groups; the location of groups). The Type 3
  groups sometimes keep the name 'nurture group', or are claimed to show
  similarities to the classic nurture group concept, but often depart
  radically from the organisational principles of classic and new type
  nurture groups (e.g. a nurture group outside of the school; one adult
  working in nurture groups). Type 3 nurture groups tend to focus on
  social and developmental issues but tend not to have the academic
  emphasis of the classic and new variant groups. Type 4 nurture groups
  claim the name 'nurture group', but do not exhibit the philosophical or
  organisational characteristics of classic nurture groups, and therefore are
  misnamed.

- Overall, the nurture group students improved in their social, emotional
  and behavioural functioning. The nurture group students' improvements
  were greater than the comparison students who were not attending the
  nurture groups. The greatest improvements were recorded during the
  initial stages of students' experiences of placing in nurture groups (e.g.
  between school terms one and two).

- Established nurture groups (those having been in existence for more than
  two years) were more effective in meeting students' social, emotional and
  behavioural needs than the newly established groups.

- The analysis of the Boxall Profile suggested nurture group students
  showed significant improvements between school terms one and two.
  The improvements between terms one and three were also significant on
  all Boxall scores. However, the differences between term two and three

scores on the whole were less significant. Whilst improvements in social, emotional and behavioural difficulties tend to be most marked between terms one and two, improvements in behaviour associated with engagement with learning tasks continues, for nurture group students, over all three periods.

- The time that nurture group students spend in nurture groups, the balance and stability of the group, and nurture group students' fluency in English appear to be salient contributory factors to the success of nurture groups.

CHAPTER 7

Involving Carers in Nurture Groups

INTRODUCTION

In this chapter we explore some of the things that carers of children in nurture groups might do to help their children do well both at school and in the home. When we talk about children 'doing well' we are thinking about the child's overall development. A child who feels safe and secure and gets on well with other people will be in a good position to get the best out of school in terms of his or her academic learning and personal development as a happy, enquiring individual. Schools can only contribute so much to helping children develop in these ways. The child will make the best use of opportunities provided by the school if the experiences he or she has outside of the school, particularly in the home, are geared towards preparing the child for what the school is trying to do.

A CHILD'S BASIC NEEDS

All human beings have basic needs for clean air, food, shelter and warmth. Whilst it may be possible to live with poor air quality, poor nutrition and inadequate shelter (Maslow 1970), it is probably the case that in these circumstances life itself would be of poor quality and of shorter duration than it would have been if these needs were more fully met. These physical needs are relatively easy to identify, if not always easy to satisfy. However, the psychological needs of humans are complex. In this chapter, we devote our attention to exploring the basic psychological needs of children and provide suggestions on how to meet them within everyday situations. Major sources of insight here are the work of Pringle (1975) and Bowlby (1969, 1980). We draw on these sources heavily throughout this chapter.

THE VITAL IMPORTANCE OF EARLY RELATIONSHIPS

All through our lives, our relationships with other people are of enormous importance to us. So much of what we think about ourselves is based on what we believe others think about us.

A child's need for love and security

From birth, carers show their affection and love through physical contact, cuddling, holding and with other verbal and non-verbal expressions. They protect their children and gradually introduce them to the social world. Within a loving relationship, the child develops feelings of self-worth and personal identity (Pringle 1975). This gives them the feeling that their existence matters to their carers, they are loved and valued. Loved children are more likely to be emotionally secure and happy. They are also more likely to show affection to others and recognise and respond to affection shown by others (*ibid*.).

Security relates to the consistency and predictability of the physical and social environment that children live in. By security we mean the consistency and continuity in care and support that carers provide, a more or less same daily routine. Children also need guidance on what is expected of them, in other words the consistency and predictability in carers' expectations and rules. When the standards of expectations and behaviours are communicated well, children are more likely to feel secure and therefore the business of raising a child becomes less stressful for carers (Pringle 1975).

Love and security are two crucial conditions for the healthy psychological development of children (Pringle 1975). The extent to which children perceive love and security can also have a crucial effect on how they view themselves. This has a direct effect on children's psychological health, in that they may develop constructive or destructive attitudes toward themselves and/or others depending on how much love and care they experience (*ibid*.). This in turn is likely to have a long-term impact on how individuals relate to their peers throughout the lifespan.

When children do not have their needs for love and security met, the needs do not go away (Bowlby 1969). Such children will express these unmet needs in different ways. Some children will appear to be overly dependent and clinging to their carers, as if constantly pleading with their carer 'please love me'. On the other hand, some children will reveal the same needs through hostile and rejecting behaviour, as if saying to their carers: 'the more that you fail to love me, the more I will try to bully you into loving me'. Other children might express these unmet needs by appearing to be without feelings. These children may appear to be completely detached from and uninterested in the people and things around them. Children in this situation appear to be saying: 'I don't know how to get my carer to love me, but I know that without that love I am unable to function. It is best for me to do nothing rather than risk doing things that may remind me that I am not loved.'

It follows that when children feel that they are safe and secure, and loved, unconditionally, they are able to become more independent of their carers. The more secure the children feel, the more confidence they have for exploring the world around them (Bowlby 1969). It also means that such children are more likely to be more confident in opening themselves up to new experiences (Pringle 1975) and to be more brave and skilful in dealing with unexpected situations. These children seem to be saying to their carers:

> Thank you for loving me and making me feel safe. I feel good about myself because I can see myself as you see me. No matter where I am or what I am doing, I always have these feelings of warmth and safety that you have given me. My duty to you is to make good use of what you have given me. I will do this by going out into the world as a loving, confident and independent person, who is able to take on challenges, get along with other people, and take responsibility for my own actions.

The human journey that we have just outlined starts from a position of dependency. When the journey goes well, the individual has his or her dependency needs met, and in so doing gathers the resources he or she needs to become independent. This is not an easy journey even when it goes well. For the carer, who invests so much of him or herself in loving and creating a secure environment for the child, the experience of the child becoming less dependent can be emotionally very difficult to handle. However, most carers realise how important it is for their child to be given freedom and opportunities for independence. On the other hand, from the child's perspective, it is often necessary to help the carer to 'let go'. This often happens during the adolescent years when the child is caught between being a child and an adult, and rebels against attempts by the carer to treat him or her as a child (Erikson 1963). Such conflict is, of course, both healthy and necessary. The end product of such conflict, if it is handled well, is a new kind of relationship between the carer and the young adult. This relationship is marked by mutual respect and the observation of adult boundaries by both parties.

When needs for love and security are not met early in life, the child will experience the world as a hostile and unpredictable place. This can seriously hamper the course of a child's healthy psychological development. As we have noted above, children express difficulties of these kinds in a variety of ways, including aggression, anger and apparent hatred, as well as through withdrawn behaviour. When the child reaches school, these problems can become amplified (Patterson *et al.* 1992). Some of these children will be unable to control and manage their anger effectively; therefore they are more likely to be labelled as 'disruptive' and 'uncooperative' in their schools (Pringle 1975). Others will simply not engage with their peers or with school work. These children are at great risk of passing unnoticed. In either case, if not dealt with in an effective and timely manner, serious problems of a social, behavioural and emotional nature may develop during the teenage and adult years.

We can conclude that a lack of love and security can have very serious consequences. It is also the case, however, that well-meaning but misguided efforts by carers to treat the child as though he or she were still at the dependency stage, when they are beyond it, are also potentially seriously damaging. In these circumstances, it becomes hard for children to escape from this emotional net. The effect of this is to hinder the development of social and emotional independence.

It is, therefore, important for carers to create a balance between meeting dependency needs, whilst allowing space for the child to experience independence. As we have already noted, the child will often be in a good position to indicate when there is a problem of this kind. This will often take the form of conflict between the carer and the child that, if handled well, will lead to a resolution that will be acceptable to both parties.

A child's need for new experiences

Personal and intellectual development depends on taking on new and often challenging experiences that the child has to make sense of (Pringle 1975). By new experiences, we imply a broad range of experiences. They could be related to school learning, such as reading, writing and drawing. They could involve exploring the outside world through play. Or they could be new socialising experiences, such as starting a new team sport. Clearly, these experiences can be solitary or shared. What is common to all of these is their newness, and the way in which this can be linked to curiosity and enjoyment.

Engaging in new experiences is one major stepping stone in the healthy development of children's minds. Feelings of achievement can also help the development of children's confidence and self-esteem. Carers can support this process by providing opportunities for their children to take on new experiences.

Play as a medium for new learning experience

From the earliest period of babyhood throughout the life span, play provides very important opportunities for children to engage with new experiences. Imagine a child is playing with sand and soil. Here is an opportunity for the young child to compare and contrast these two materials by feeling and seeing, in a situation that is guided solely by the child's desire for exploration and stimulation. Another example could be when children play co-operatively, such as in a shopping game. Here they take on the different roles of shopkeeper and customer and act out the social rituals that they have observed in real shops. This can be an excellent opportunity for sharing and developing communication and self-expression skills which are very important not only in school life but throughout adult life. An inherent feature of play is that it is enjoyable. There is no greater motivation for carrying on an activity than pleasure. This is why play is a central feature of nurture group practice, as we have already noted in previous chapters.

An important thing to bear in mind is the way in which we commonly think about play as a childish and trivial activity. For example, we tend to draw a distinction between 'work' and 'play'. Work is seen as serious and important, whilst play is seen as providing a break from work. Ironically, it is not uncommon for adults to see their 'work' (i.e. their paid employment) as a means of financing their play (i.e. hobbies and other personal interests). In fact, most of us require external motivation, usually in the form of money, to continue working, whilst we 'play' simply for the joy of playing.

From an educational point of view, however, the intrinsic motivation that is associated with play is an excellent means of engaging pupils in learning activities. Skilled teachers learn very quickly which kinds of play activities can be exploited for educational purposes. So, far from it being the case that 'work' is more important than 'play', the most effective forms of school work often involve elements of play.

An additional important point here is that when children are playing they are often engaging in important learning activities. Sometimes these activities involve practising or rehearsing particular skills (e.g. role-playing conversations between two dolls; constructing shapes from building blocks). It is a good idea to encourage children in this kind of activity, even when it may appear to be inconvenient (e.g. creating a mess in the living room; the child's clothes getting dirty). Helping a child to feel that play is important and valuable is likely to contribute positively to the child's development.

It is not hard to imagine a mother or father stopping their child from playing with paint or mud or clay because the room gets dirty. If the child becomes excited and makes a mess out of the material that she or he is playing with, disapproval or even punishment may cause the child to feel guilty and/or fearful. It will be educationally very harmful for a child to associate exploration and experimentation with feelings of guilt and/or fear. This is not to say that children should be given unlimited freedom to play when and where and with what they choose. Adults, however, need to be very careful about how they set boundaries for children's play. It is very important, for example, for children to have access to a space and materials (e.g. toys) that they feel ownership of (Pringle 1975).

It is very important for opportunities to be created when adults and children can play together. Not only is this enjoyable in itself, and therefore important to the developing adult–child relationship, it is also through play of this kind that adults can help to structure new learning experiences for the child.

One of the most important features of play is imagination. Carers and teachers do not need access to expensive toys and equipment in order to create stimulating play activities. Simple everyday objects, such as cooking utensils, cardboard boxes and old clothes, can be the basis for extremely engaging games, as can play with words and stories. The crucial feature of adult–child play is shared engagement in an enjoyable activity. As such it is the relationship between the adult and the child that is important rather than the play objects.

A child's need for praise and recognition

Going through childhood is not an easy business. Whilst new experiences can be exciting and enjoyable, they can also be challenging. Challenges can be stimulating, but they can also be threatening. An important role for the adult is to help the child deal with this difficult period by giving him or her support and encouragement (Pringle 1975). Recognition of the child's effort and progress, and praise for his or her achievements, however small these achievements may be, are very important ways of motivating the child. It is through praise and recognition that children learn the value that others put on what they do. This praise and recognition then becomes internalised, so that the child comes to know when they are doing things that are praiseworthy. This is the basis for positive self-esteem.

It is very important that the praise and recognition are given to children in ways that enable the child to understand why they are receiving such attention. If praise and recognition are given without explanation, or inconsistently (e.g. the child is praised for behaviour on Monday that is ignored or disapproved of on Tuesday), the child may well appreciate the praise and recognition, but may find it more difficult to associate this with their own behaviour, and may simply see the praise and recognition as something that is given out at the whim of the adult. This is not a good situation from the child's point of view, because it is confusing, and fails to give the child a sense of how they might, through their own efforts, encourage the adult to give them praise in the future, by choosing to repeat behaviour that has already been praised. When adults praise children, therefore, their praise statements should usually be in two parts:

1.   the praise statement (e.g. 'well done')

2.   an explanation for the praise (e.g. 'you have painted a very colourful picture').

It is important to note that in some schools praise and recognition are made available only for a very narrow range of children's performance. Where this is the case, academic achievement is often favoured over other kinds of performance (e.g. social behaviour). When praising children, an important consideration should be the focus of the praise. How children approach their learning and how much effort they put into their work should also be recognised, as well as how well they co-operate with others.

Praise and recognition can serve a number of functions in supporting a child's healthy psychological development. First of all, it leads to a sense of self-esteem: seeing a desirable image of oneself in the eyes of others. A positive self-image also helps the development of the sense of adequacy, not only in childhood but also through adult life (Pringle 1975). Adults can also use praise appropriately to emphasise the desired behaviour, which appears to be a powerful way of supporting the child's behavioural development. However, in order for this approach to work, it is very important to pay attention to what we praise and how much we praise.

All children are different. This brings us to the issue of how much the use of praise and recognition might vary in relation to the individual child's needs. Children with emotional difficulties or low self-esteem may need more intensive praise and recognition than other children (Pringle 1975).

Of course, not all children's behaviour is worthy of positive recognition and praise. When a child is used to having their positive behaviour praised and recognised, the absence of praise and recognition can be a powerful indicator to the child that a particular behaviour is not desirable. It is for this reason that a child's negative behaviour can sometimes be modified through being ignored by the adult. Ignoring, however, is most likely to have this effect if it is experienced by the child as the withholding of praise and recognition. To put it another way, how can a child be expected to know that being ignored is a sign of disapproval if they have not had considerable experience of having their positive behaviour acknowledged and actively approved?

Most psychologists would agree that it is important, usually, to avoid drawing attention to bad behaviour. Recognition, after all, is a form of attention, and attention can be a powerful form of reinforcement. It is positive behaviour, of course, that should be the focus of reinforcement. Even a negative acknowledgement of a child's bad behaviour can act as a source of recognition. This is especially the case for the child who seldom receives positive attention for his or her good behaviour.

Having said this, there are times when it is not possible or desirable to ignore the child's negative behaviour, especially when the child behaves in ways that are offensive or potentially harmful to other people, or themselves. Here, the same principle applies as does to praise. When a child is reprimanded for bad behaviour, the adult giving the reprimand must always explain clearly why the reprimand is necessary. Once again, it is very important to remember that reprimands are most effective in changing behaviour when the child is aware from experience that the person giving the reprimand is also a major source of praise and positive recognition.

As is often the case, as many carers and school staff will know, using praise is not as straightforward as it may sometimes sound. It is, for example, counter-productive to use praise indiscriminately. If a child receives praise for everything he or she does then praise may lose its value for the child. As a result, praise will have limited impact on the child's behaviour. The art of using praise and recognition well is to be *consistent*, but at the same time *selective*. This means that the adult has to think very carefully about what they are giving praise for and why they are giving it. Praise should be given for the behaviour that the adult wants the child to repeat, because that behaviour is likely to make a positive contribution to the child's social, emotional and/or cognitive development.

It is widely understood that rewards can be used to shape and improve a child's behaviour. Adults can use rewards very effectively as ways of encouraging children to repeat specific behaviours. When we talk about rewards, however, we are not necessarily referring to expensive presents or objects of any kind. A reward is a symbol of praise and recognition. For many children, simply being told that their behaviour is praiseworthy is a sufficient reward, so long as the reason for the praise is made clear. Though it clearly does no harm to use more concrete rewards from time to time in order to bring variety into the situation.

A child's need for responsibility

The last need of children identified by Pringle (1975), and probably the most neglected, is the need for responsibility. Developing children's sense of responsibility is actually about developing children's judgement, autonomy and eventually their independence. Developing children's sense of responsibility means developing their insightful judgements about their own feelings and motives so that they can make wise decisions. Here, an important point is that children develop the notion that there are choices in life, and that different choices will have different consequences.

Children who repeatedly behave in ways that upset other people as well as themselves often have a very loose grip on the relationship between their behaviour and its consequences for themselves and others. This lack of awareness puts the child at severe risk of being disengaged from their social environment and perhaps being rejected by their peers (and others). Furthermore, this lack of awareness can be associated with coercive and anti-social behaviour towards others, and with social rejection.

Having accepted the importance of developing a sense of responsibility in children, we will now explore some of the ways in which adults might help facilitate the development of such a sense of responsibility.

Adults can help children develop a sense of responsibility by enabling them to understand that they have choices in how they behave. Here again finding a balanced approach is important. Young children need a framework of expectations, which can help them to guide their own actions. For example, in the home situation, the accepted rules of the family home need to be communicated to children in a clear and accessible way. The same thing is true of the school setting. Without a clear framework, it is much harder for the child to learn what is acceptable and unacceptable behaviour. In these circumstances, the child will only learn through a process of trial and error. By having a clear set of rules, which are few in number and expressed in simple terms, the child is given a clear indication of what they might do in order to receive recognition and praise. These rules should be attached to key features of daily routines (e.g. getting up in the morning; meal times; preparing to leave the home for school; greetings and farewells; bedtimes). They should also be simple rules, for example 'always wash and clean teeth in the morning and before bed'; 'during meal times, always sit at the table and be friendly to others'; 'always go to bed at a set time during the school term'; 'always get up in the morning at a set time during the school term'.

Adults need to be very careful about the rigidity of the rules that are used. Clearly, some rules are not open to negotiation; for example, it is perfectly reasonable for the carer to insist that a child should be at home before a certain time in the afternoon or evening, or that they should avoid dangerous areas (e.g. railway lines, busy roads). Even in these circumstances, it is very important that the reason for the rule be made clear to the child. After all, the main purpose of setting rules for the child is for rules to influence the child's behaviour, as a result of the child *choosing* to abide by the rules.

This emphasis on choice means that the negotiation of rules, where appropriate, can be a very important aid to selecting rules that work. If a child is involved in discussing and creating a particular rule, he or she is more likely to understand its importance and its logic and, therefore, abide by it. On the other hand, when discipline is only a matter of carers', or other people's, rules and directions, the child will find it difficult to exercise his or her own judgement and responsibility. A child-oriented approach requires inviting children to talk about their own behaviour and actions and inviting them to generate solutions to potential problems. Rules, therefore, should always be seen as sensible solutions to potentially serious problems.

It would be unreasonable for adults to expect children to develop a sense of responsibility instantly. This is a gradual, developmental process. However, even from a very young age, children can be given certain spheres of responsibility. For example, one would expect children at an early stage, after they have been successfully potty trained, to make the transition to using the adult toilet. At first, this would involve the child in drawing an adult's attention to their desire to use the toilet. Eventually, the child will be able to do this without adult help or supervision. This is a clear example of the way in which most children gradually take increasing amounts of responsibility for their behaviour. It would be very unreasonable to expect the child to use adult facilities without adult supervision in the initial stages. The same principle applies to other areas of responsibility. Individual responsibility often follows from shared responsibility.

The adult's role is to support the child initially through the sharing of tasks, before passing full responsibility for a particular issue over to the child. Sometimes, the child will tell the adult when they are ready to take on a particular responsibility themselves. At other times, the adult will make a judgement based upon their observation and knowledge of the child that it is now time to give the child the opportunity to shoulder a particular responsibility. For example, there comes a stage in many children's experience of going to school when they no longer require their carer to take them to their classroom. At first, the child may indicate that they do not wish to be accompanied beyond the entrance to the school building; later the child may extend this to the school gate. Eventually, the child may indicate that they no longer wish to be accompanied on the journey to school. On the other hand, another child might continue to 'allow' his or her carer to accompany them to the classroom long after they feel confident enough to proceed to the classroom alone. It is, therefore, through processes of observation and negotiation that the child's scope for personal responsibility is gradually extended. Sometimes it will be the case that the child's desire for independence will exceed what the adult believes to be the bounds of safety and reasonableness. Obviously, it is the carer's responsibility to ensure the child's safety and well-being at all costs. However, there are times when it is appropriate for the adult to initiate a situation in which a child is given the opportunity to take on a particular responsibility.

When a child reaches school age, there is sometimes a gap between the extent to which a child is ready to take on personal responsibilities in certain areas, and the expectations of the school. Not only that, but it is commonly the case that the expectations that schools have in this regard increase as the child passes from one year group to the next. For example, as school pupils get older, they are expected to take increasing responsibility in relation to schoolwork and school-based routines. It is important, however, that schools and teachers do not impose such expectations without creating opportunities for children to receive support in extending their scope for personal responsibility. This will often mean building into the school curriculum opportunities for children to exercise choice and to explore and understand the consequences of their own and others' behaviour.

These opportunities should be consistently available in the kinds of formal learning activities that take place in classrooms, as well as in the social dimension of school life (e.g. as reflected in school codes and policies for conduct and behaviour). Here, the point is that unless children are given different options for behaviour, they will find it difficult to exercise the intensely important skill of personal decision-making.

SUMMARY

In this chapter, we explored the psychological needs of children.

A central feature here is the need for warm, empathic, supportive and nurturing relationships between children and their carers. The more that children experience this kind of relationship, the more they will grow and develop psychologically healthy ways. The psychologically healthy person is one who is self-knowing, self-confident, sociable, co-operative and self-directing.

CHAPTER 8

A Model for Analysing Problem Situations: SALAD

THE SALAD CONCEPT

In the previous chapter, we explored children's needs and addressed the possible consequences of their needs being unmet. In this part of the book, we will explore a framework developed by Olsen and Cooper (2001), designed to analyse situations where disruptive behaviour appears to occur, and identify opportunities for intervention. This can be used both by school staff and carers. This framework has five key areas. These are Systems, Access, Limits, Acceptance and Direction. The framework is based on the idea that behavioural difficulties often stem from problems in the relationships *between* carers, children and schools rather than from within individuals. An important objective of the SALAD framework is to identify patterns of interaction between people that create and/or keep problems going, and ways in which these patterns might be altered. The approach draws on social systems theory (Von Bertalanffy 1968) and the applications of this theory to the social/interpersonal domain (Bateson 1972; Hoffman 1981) and educational situations (Cooper and Upton 1990; Jones 1995).

SYSTEMS

The word 'system' is used here in the same way that it is used in biology. In biology we talk about eco-systems. An eco-system is a finely balanced living environment in which each organism depends on all the other organisms for their own survival. Human social systems can be seen to operate in very similar ways. On the one hand, we depend upon those people we interact with regularly to meet our needs for security, affiliation and esteem. In turn, they depend upon us to have the same needs met. Human relationships, therefore, can be thought of as *transactional*; that is, defined by a process of exchange. One of the problems with any transactional relation is the importance of the value of the items that are exchanged between the participants in the relationship. Because we have to give something, in order to receive what we want from a relationship, there is always the danger that one member of the relationship may be being 'short changed', so that he or she is giving more than he or she is receiving in return. This creates the potential for conflict that is inherent in any relationship. Conflict does not always involve problems of relative values, but can also be created when members of a relationship have competing requirements. For example, things go well when one person in a relationship feels that they need to be comforted and the other person is in a position to offer comfort and is willing to do so. However, when both individuals are in need of comfort at the same time, there may be a problem, especially if neither individual feels able to take the role of the comforter.

If we take the systems analogy further we also have to acknowledge that what goes on in the two-person subsystem has an influence on and is influenced by other relationships, which each member of that two-person subsystem has with other people (i.e. outside of that subsystem). For example, the relationship between a mother and daughter could be influenced by the relationship the child has with her father. Similarly, the kind of relationships that the daughter has with her peers and adults she meets in the school will influence the way she relates to the people within the family situation, and so on. A systems perspective, therefore, attempts to capture the complex web of interacting relationships that human beings engage in.

To put systems in a practical context, let us imagine a student who presents challenging behaviour at home. If we want to analyse this situation by using a systemic approach, we need to look at all of the different influences that may have an impact on the observed behaviour. From a systemic perspective, we can suggest that what happens at home is affected by what happens in the classroom. Also, what happens in the classroom is affected by what happens at home.

A crucial starting point for working within this framework is an understanding of how a problem situation is defined. In social situations, we generally deal with a number of people with different standpoints and motivations. Challenging situations and tensions may arise if people only view situations from their own perspectives and fail in trying to understand others' points of view and motivations. In order to put this into context, let us imagine a nurture group student who shows some problematic behaviour in his or her mainstream classroom by disturbing other students. In this situation, the headteacher, the class teacher, the psychologist, the carers and the child may interpret the situation differently, as shown in Table 8.1.

Table 8.1: The blame cycle

Mainstream teacher	'The NG teacher is supposed to improve this behaviour. I need to focus on my teaching and students' learning and I should not have to experience these situations.'
Nurture group teacher	'The student is quiet and does not show such behaviour in my class. It is really, really rare.'
Carer	'I just wish the school could learn to handle these problems on their own without phoning us. Why don't they just use the cane? It never did me any harm. He is just a bit of a naughty boy sometimes – that is all.'
Student	'The teacher does not like me at all. She never bothers about my work.'
Headteacher	'If the classroom teacher had interesting lessons, there'd be no discipline problems; good teachers don't seek outside help for behaviour management problems in their own classrooms.'
Psychologist	'I give these teachers all of these ideas but they never bother to use them.'

Based on Olsen and Cooper 2001

Table 8.1 provides a good example of how different interpretations of the same situation create a *blame cycle*. When every stakeholder (i.e. each person involved in the various related subsystems, such as family and the school) blames the rest for what is happening and fails to take responsibility for any influence they may have on the problem situation, the chances of helping the student who experiences the difficulties are seriously decreased. Therefore, it is important to find ways of removing the blame from individuals and finding common ground on which stakeholders can begin to agree and co-operate. Table 8.2 summarises the first step in reconstructing perceptions of a problem situation.

Table 8.2: Reconstructing perceptions of a problem situation (1)

STEP 1: Remove the barriers from the relationships between different stakeholders

- Stop blaming others for the cause and maintenance of the problem situation.
- Do not expect others to fix the problem alone.
- Try to empathise with others (i.e. try to view the problem from the perspective of other people involved in the situation).

When we empathise with others with whom we have fallen out, we often remove barriers from our relationships with them that have prevented a positive solution being reached. Once we empathise, we should be able to find a solution that is agreeable to both parties. For example, school staff need to be sensitive to the family's values and ideas, and acknowledge carers as 'co-workers' who have a vested interest in improving the situation. So, rather than focusing on negative behaviour, and linking this to the home situation, school staff need to focus on solutions and discuss these with carers. By approaching carers in this co-operative way, the natural defensive reactions that they might at first feel, when confronted with tales of their child's misbehaviour, are made unnecessary. Rather, the carer is being invited to share in the search for a solution that will benefit him or her, the child and the school. Furthermore, the school is accepting that there may be things that staff can and should do to address the problem.

Also, carers need to listen to the school's observations and try to understand their interpretations of the situation. For carers, it may not always be easy to talk about challenging situations, especially if there is a problem with their child's behaviour that they feel unable to deal with. The old saying 'a problem shared is a problem halved' is very relevant here. By listening to others' ways of thinking about the problem, the carer may begin to develop new insight into the problem and thus move closer to a solution. This process of developing a new way of thinking about a problem situation is sometimes referred to as 're-framing' (see Table 8.3). The crucial point is that whatever school staff and carers have to say about the problem should always be constructive, which means that it should always be directed towards finding a solution, rather than simply reinforcing the idea that the problem cannot be solved.

Also, carers can help school staff by informing them about their own observations of the problem situation and discuss any suggested plan for improvement. In some cases, a caseworker (i.e. a school-based behaviour consultant or support worker) can unite different stakeholders by enabling communication between carers and staff that is non-argumentative and respectful of both parties.

Having explored the problem from different stakeholders' points of view, it is important to reflect back upon the problem again. Table 8.3 illustrates key issues around re-framing.

For effective change the stakeholders need to work collaboratively towards a common goal. Each stakeholder has the job of tackling the problem in their own situation (e.g. carers at home, teachers at school). It is important, however, that these different stakeholders are in effective communication with each other to ensure that they are working to the same ends. This means that regular communication between carers and school staff is a very important feature of good staff–carer relations. Table 8.4 summarises the key issues around the concept of joint work.

Table 8.3: Reconstructing perceptions of a problem situation (2)

STEP 2: Re-framing the problem

- The aim of re-framing is to escape from ways of thinking about problem behaviour that do not contribute to changing the behaviour. Such negative ways of thinking actually help to *maintain* the problem.

- When we re-frame problem behaviour we deliberately find new and more positive explanations for the behaviour. In other words, we try to see the behaviour as a practical and understandable solution to another problem.

  > E.g. a child who persistently disrupts lessons through shouting out might at first be thought to be doing this deliberately. This behaviour, however, might be re-framed more positively as the child's over-enthusiasm and desire to perform well in the lesson. This makes the behaviour nobody's fault. The job of the carers and the school staff, rather than being to blame one another for not controlling the child effectively, becomes one of 1. communicating to the child the re-framing of his or her behaviour, and 2. co-operating to find ways in which the child's enthusiasm might be harnessed and rewarded both in the family and school setting. Though, of course, it would be indicated to the child that there are much better ways of having his or her enthusiasm acknowledged and rewarded than shouting out in class.

- The advantage of this approach is that it replaces conflict with co-operation: staff, carers and the child are placed in a situation in which they are all working towards the same goal. The act of co-operation, in itself, can change the whole tone of this three-way relationship, thus removing anger and frustration that may have been at the root of the original problem.

- It is important when new explanations for problem behaviour are being created, for re-framing purposes, that they should not be too unusual or outlandish to the stakeholders. Though, having said this, a slightly unusual explanation can sometimes be very powerful in helping people to see things in new ways. One of the reasons why this approach often works is that problem behaviour is not always based on rational decision-making, and is often as distressing to the person carrying out the behaviour as it is to everyone else. By giving the individual a positive, rational reason for behaviour that is out of everyone's control, an opportunity is created that enables the individual to stop the unwanted behaviour by finding alternative ways of achieving the newly defined reasons for the unwanted behaviour. Obviously, there are times when children behave badly for very clear and rational reasons. These circumstances would be handled differently. Re-framing is most appropriate when no such genuine rational explanation can be found.

- In developing re-frames, it is important for school staff to acknowledge and respect the family's culture, values and beliefs.

Table 8.4: Recreating a climate of co-operation

STEP 3: Carers and school staff working towards a common goal

Carers	*School staff*
• Attend school meetings.	• Do not impose solutions.
• Do not hesitate to contact the school to inform staff of how things are going with you and your child.	• Acknowledge family values.
	• Establish a positive and welcoming environment.
• Be active in generating solutions, and avoid blaming yourself.	• When feeding back information to parents, recognise child's strengths as well as the areas for improvement.
• Avoid blaming school staff where possible unless that is the only *possible* explanation.	• Use a non-specialist language to maintain communication.
• Avoid blaming the child.	• Do not de-skill carers by undermining their parenting skills.

ACCESS

The first **A** in SALAD refers to Access. As students become older, they start engaging with a wider social network. In particular, when they start school children begin spending much more time with their peers and adults who are from outside their family or neighbourhood. Immediately they start school they are expected to be able to co-operate with their peers, and to respond positively to the expectations of the school staff. This means students need to learn to regulate their own behaviour, and develop and maintain positive links with peers and school staff. The older the child gets, the higher the expectation that they will be able to manage effectively conflict with others. The concept of *access* and its reinforcement within the family and school environment can be helpful for students to cope with a number of social situations.

When we talk about 'access' in this context, we are referring to the need that the child has to have access to knowledge of what behaviour and behavioural standards are expected of him or her (Olsen and Cooper 2001). Key to this definition is developing students' *ownership* of their behaviour, including problem situations and their solutions. Carers and school staff can help children to develop their ownership and sense of responsibility.

Crucial to the development of students' ownership and sense of responsibility over their behaviour is the communication of social expectations, routines and rules. Having a secure environment where students have a clear understanding of rules and routine can also help foster this development. Target setting can be a very helpful way of communicating expectations and monitoring the progress towards meeting these goals. Figure 8.1 summarises the key features of the 'access' concept.

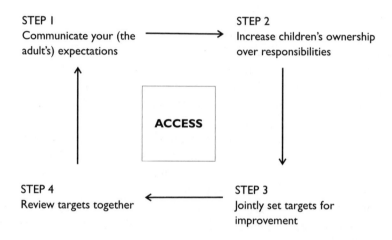

Figure 8.1: Key features of the access concept

Before we show how the access model can be put into practice, Table 8.5 shows two issues that carers and school staff could reflect upon (Olsen and Cooper 2001).

1. Communication of expectations

Table 8.5 points out the need for carers and teachers to be very clear in the way in which they communicate to children how they wish and expect them to behave. Without a clear indication of this kind, children may find themselves confused, and therefore have difficulties in selecting an appropriate behaviour.

Table 8.5: Access to expectations

Key issues to test your child/student's access to expectations

- Discuss with the child what kinds of positive behaviours are expected in the home and school.

- Increase your child's awareness of what he or she needs to do in order to improve his or her behaviour.

There are different ways that carers and school staff can communicate and reinforce expectations and desired behaviour. Discussions with students can play an important role. The most useful discussions will take place within the context of what has happened or is currently happening, rather than in relation to what might happen (Olsen and Cooper 2001). This means that the carers should look out for opportunities that arise within daily routines to point out the kinds of behaviours that are required. For example, carers can ask their children to repeat important house rules to friends of the child who might visit. This will reinforce the rules for the child. We should never underestimate the need for rules to be re-stated and reinforced. Over time this reinforcement will lead to the child taking ownership of a commitment to rules.

The communication of expectations is the starting point in the process of teaching a child self-discipline, that is the child's ability to regulate his or her own behaviour.

2. Developing children's ownership

When students are encouraged to participate in rule-setting and other kinds of decision making, they are more likely to feel motivated to comply with these rules and decisions than if the rules and decisions are simply imposed upon them. Also, a further effect of participation of this kind is that it encourages the child to feel that he or she has an important role in the family and school and that their involvement has consequences. In other words, they learn that what they think and what they do can cause change to happen. If children do not have these positive experiences of seeing the consequences of their thinking and behaviour, they are unlikely to be able to understand the consequences of their negative behaviour. Children who only learn about the consequences of their behaviour when they are negative are likely to develop a distorted impression of themselves as 'bad' people. It is much better for the child's self-esteem to learn about the way in which their behaviour has consequences through the experience of positive consequences.

The quality of the relationship between adults (carers and school staff) and children can either help or hinder the development of children's sense of ownership. If an adult simply tells a child what kind of behaviour is required, there is no guarantee that the child really understands what is required. Some children will be obedient regardless of whether or not they understand the command they are obeying. This kind of blind obedience, however, is superficial and is not likely to contribute to the development of self-regulation. The kind of ownership that we have talked about in this section is a product of genuine two-way communication between adult and child in which the child's understandings are as important as those of the adult.

3. Target and rule-setting for improvement: Knowing what to do

Children need to be guided towards desired behaviour. Effective communication and target setting in a family or classroom can help children to recognise their responsibilities as well as provide them with a direction to move forward to. If children are encouraged to participate in this process, they may feel more in control of their own behaviour. Once children understand and contribute to deciding about the next steps, adults need to support and monitor them to achieve those goals. The pointers in Table 8.6 could be helpful to adults for evaluating the target-setting process.

Table 8.6: Target and rule-setting for improvement

Target-setting: Some key issues

- Discuss the next steps with your child.
- Make sure that the target is reasonable and achievable.
- Explain how a specific target relates to your family/classroom routines and common goals.
- Demonstrate to your child how he or she might work towards his or her target.
- Discuss the potential consequences of not meeting the target.

The nature of communication between adults and children is crucial for effective target-setting. Through discussions adults can make children aware of a specific problem situation and ask them to generate ideas on how to solve it. Even if there is not a commonly agreed solution in the end, discussions can help children to become aware of a need to change.

We have already stressed the importance of increasing children's involvement in the target and rule-setting processes. One way of achieving this could be to play a game with the child which involves 1. identifying a problem situation (e.g. what happens if somebody steals your dinner money at school?), and 2. taking turns to think of as many different ways of behaving to improve that situation. Then the best ideas could be discussed in terms of their possible consequences. Role-plays could also be helpful in demonstrating what it looks like and feels like when a particular behavioural target is reached (e.g. when the child has succeeded in preparing for school in the mornings on time, for three days in a row). In such activities, different scenarios can be acted out and discussed in terms of consequences and feelings (Kitson 2006).

4. Monitoring and reviewing improvement

Monitoring and communication are very important elements in systemic strategies for facilitating positive change in children's behaviour. Children can be encouraged to assess their own behaviour, and this in turn can help them to develop a deep understanding of rules and targets and their importance. Adults can help children to self-monitor by taking opportunities to engage in the kind of activities that we have talked about in the last paragraph.

When a desired behaviour is achieved, adults can actually talk about why such behaviour matters to them, and praise their children for being sensible and wise. On the other hand, when children behave in undesirable ways, adults can still reflect back upon the undesired behaviour and explore the consequences and feelings and focus on other positive behaviour.

Another reason why children need to have access to knowledge of what is desirable behaviour is the need to know what is undesirable. In the following section, we will look at this idea within the concept of *limits*.

LIMITS

The **L** in SALAD refers to Limits. An important part of what carers and school staff can do to support children's development during the early and middle years involves control and monitoring strategies. This can be thought of in terms of setting limits.

Setting limits for children involves the communication of what is and what is not acceptable behaviour at home and in school. When the limits are clear, children are more likely to feel secure and be able to work co-operatively with carers and school staff. Where limits are clearly defined, they also provide good opportunities for adults to judge the extent to which the child has developed the power of self-control. In this way, 'limits' help us to monitor a child's progress and development. Table 8.7 summarises the benefits of setting limits in supporting children's development.

Table 8.7: Benefits of limits

- Limits define what is acceptable and unacceptable behaviour.
- Limits and routines provide children with a secure and predictable family and school environment.
- Children internalise these limits and use them to help develop their own powers of self-control and self-regulation.
- Setting limits implies a *preventive* strategy rather than a *reactive* one.
- Having a common understanding of rules, responsibilities and limits provides carers, teachers and children with tools to analyse problem situations more effectively.

Limits can be thought of as behavioural boundaries. A boundary is a line which should not be crossed, because to cross it is to produce undesirable consequences. Therefore, limits should be thought of as being clearly justifiable on the grounds that they serve everyone's interests. For example, if a child does not observe road safety rules, he or she is at risk of injury. On the other hand, if a child engages in behaviour that is dangerous to others, then whilst there may not be an immediate physical risk to the child performing the behaviour, the social disapproval of others and guilt that the child may experience are important sources of concern for that child.

Limits and boundaries can be communicated within a family's daily routines. Most families have certain (at least, ideal) rules about the use of space and facilities in the family home. They also have expected standards of behaviour at home. There are social routines, for example, concerned with how people in the family talk to one another. There are probably important differences between how people behave with each other in the privacy of the family home, and how they are expected to behave with people who are not part of the family. Children will also have their own routines related to their school life, such as getting up at a certain time during school term, a certain time for leaving home for school, and so on. All of these routines are needed for creating a harmonious atmosphere at home. They are also helpful in the development of mutual understanding between parents and children about respective roles and responsibilities. This in turn contributes to a balanced and harmonious family life.

As with the communication of rules and targets, limits can be communicated through a number of steps. These steps are illustrated in Figure 8.2.

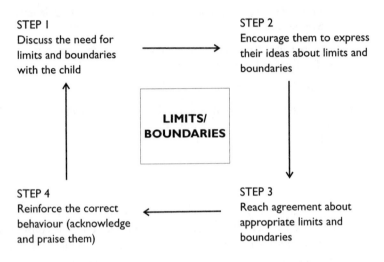

Figure 8.2: Key features of the limits concept

When setting limits and boundaries, we are not suggesting that adults should exercise total control over their children, by telling them in each stage what they should be doing and not doing. However, a child will only develop the kinds of self-control and judgement necessary to make their own decisions if they have been given clear ideas about what positive behaviour looks like, and adult support in putting these ideas into practice.

It is healthy to think in terms of gradually empowering children to develop these self-regulatory processes whereby they come to control their own behaviour. For instance, Maccoby (1984) suggested a three-stage process for the middle childhood period. In the first stage, adults supervise their children and establish and communicate rules, responsibilities, expectations and limits. Throughout childhood, children start making sense of these ideas and internalising the behavioural framework. Then they enter the process of 'co-regulation'. This is a stage shared by adult and child, in which boundaries are negotiated. The following illustrates an example of a 'co-regulatory' process involving adults and children.

With a six-year-old child, the parent sets a bedtime of 8:30 every night. After a while, the child requests that he or she would like to be allowed to stay up after this time. The reason for the 8:30 bedtime is to ensure that the child gets sufficient sleep to be wide awake on school days. It is important that the child understands this reasoning. If the child has shown the ability and willingness to understand this reasoning and has complied with the rule when required to, then it is reasonable to discuss with him or her the possible consequences to extending his or her bedtime, if the child raises the issue. For example, he or she may wish to stay up later than 8.30 in order to see a particular TV programme. It will be both necessary and fruitful to explore the consequences of approving the child's request, by discussing with the child the pros and cons of the situation. For example, on the one hand, if he or she gets to see the programme on TV, he or she may be tired the next day. If he or she is tired the next day, then this may create further negative consequences at school. The important issue here is the need to encourage the child to explore the consequences of his or her request, rather than to have them pointed out only by the adult.

This process leads to another stage, where adults decrease their control and children have more autonomy over their behaviour and choices. For example, this might mean that the child is allowed to try staying up to watch the late TV show, once or twice. However, now the responsibility is the child's and he or she has an opportunity to experience direct consequences of behaviour that they initiated. If the child has difficulties at school due to the lack of sleep, he or she should be expected to stop extending the sleeping hours. If this decision does not come from the child, the carer can intervene to prevent maintaining the negative consequences at school. Such directive intervention, however, is a last resort.

This example highlights the importance of discussion, which enables the adult and the child to explore jointly the reasoning behind the rules.

ACCEPTANCE

The second **A** in SALAD refers to Acceptance – 'to receive or welcome'. Acceptance is a crucial part of the SALAD concept. Children need acceptance within their family environments and in extra-familial contexts. Acceptance by others is a necessary element for a healthy child's psychological development.

It can be suggested that acceptance is a human social need for people of all ages. It is important for an adult to be an accepted family member (e.g. by partner and children). People also need to be respected and accepted in different social circles in which they engage (e.g. in the workplace and amongst friends). When people feel that they are not accepted in these social circles, they are seriously challenged, both psychologically and emotionally, whatever their life stage.

When children experience the absence of acceptance, there is a strong sense of hurt and rejection. Indeed, the experience (and/or perception) of rejection appears to be a major factor contributing to the development of social, emotional and behavioural problems (Olsen and Cooper 2001). The feeling of rejection is often accompanied by emotional pain, and blame for others for not being understanding and fair (Cooper 1993; Cooper et al. 2000; Olsen 1989, 1997). When adults fail to deal effectively with children's feelings of rejection, the emotional and social tension in the situation tends to escalate.

There are ways in which adults can help facilitate children's feelings of being 'accepted'. Carers and school staff can promote a warm and welcoming environment where children feel that they are a crucial part of what is going on around them and, therefore, become better positioned to develop positive relationships with others. Table 8.8 illustrates a number of ways to ensure a climate of 'acceptance' both within the school and home environment (Olsen and Cooper 2001).

Table 8.8: Development of acceptance

Preventing rejection

- Adults should not put down children in front of other peers.
- Adults should be able to apologise if necessary.
- Adults should not be judgemental when a problem situation occurs.
- Adults and children need to jointly own any problem situations.
- A solution-oriented approach is important to prevent the feelings of rejection from developing.

Table 8.8 cont.

Developing respect

- Adults should promote the development of a trustworthy and reliable way of relating to children.

- Adults should keep a consistent approach in relating to children.

- Adults should provide positive role-modelling for children.

- Adults should be fair to different children.

Enabling effective feedback

- Frequent feedback is essential to keep the communication going between adults and children.

- Adults need to prioritise what to feed back (rather than dealing with large numbers of issues).

- The circumstances in which the feedback is delivered also affects the way in which it is received by the child (e.g. in private or in front of other children).

- Feedback should not be a one-way process; children should also be encouraged to provide feedback on their own behaviour or work, as well as to others (including adults).

- Feedback should not only focus on past behaviour or work, but should be linked to the future (what the child needs to do differently for positive change).

Effective negotiation

- Children should be taught constructive negotiation skills.

- Adults should emphasise the importance of 'empathic listening' and a genuine desire to understand and appreciate others' points of view (rather than selecting what he or she wants to hear).

- Adults should encourage children to actively listen to others.

- Adults should prevent children from ignoring others' views in social negotiations.

Emphasis on feelings

- Adults should create opportunities to raise emotional awareness by encouraging children to talk about their feelings.

- Adults should help facilitate children's awareness of the ways in which their feelings interfere with their daily lives.

Table continues on next page

Table 8.8 cont.

Group work

- Group work can create opportunities for children to regulate their behaviour, and to co-operate with others.

- Group work can promote a sense of 'belonging' for the children involved.

- Adults should create opportunities for children to reflect back upon the group work processes (i.e. identifying the situations when the group is working effectively and recognising negative factors that inhibit effective collaborations).

- Adults should pay attention to the organisational aspects of group work (e.g. the size and composition of groups and allocation of time for group reflections).

Based on Olsen and Cooper 2001

DIRECTION

The **D** in SALAD refers to Direction. The last component of the SALAD framework is guiding and scaffolding children for improvement. As we have already noted, children benefit from clear guidelines (e.g. limits, boundaries, expectations and targets), because these help the child to regulate their own behaviour. We have already identified target-setting as an effective way of showing children the preferred 'direction'.

Direction can be communicated and reinforced through target-setting. Children may be more motivated if they know the target towards which they are being directed and if their success is recognised and celebrated when they reach it. We have already identified a number of issues that are important in effective target-setting in the section on 'access'. Table 8.9 illustrates some additional points that can be helpful in guiding adults' target-setting practices (Olsen and Cooper 2001).

Successful communication of 'direction' requires adults to pay attention on what targets to set, how to communicate them, and how to monitor improvement towards meeting these targets. This can be a more challenging task than it appears on the surface. For instance, one obvious problem at secondary school level is that teachers often have too many targets set at a specific time for children (Tiknaz 2004). This may confuse children in terms of what to focus on. This calls for a prioritisation for adults in their target-setting, which in turn becomes a more manageable task for children.

Table 8.9: Target-setting: Further key issues

- Jointly construct clear goals for children to improve in the areas of concern.
- Consider whether or not the goals are realistic and achievable.
- Communicate the direction to your child in a child-friendly language.
- Negotiate with your child and involve him or her in the target-setting process.
- Find ways to demonstrate and remind him or her of his or her targets.

Based on Olsen and Cooper 2001

Targets need to be communicated through a child-friendly language. Adults need to talk with children and make sure that targets actually make sense in children's everyday life. Adults can use different tools to communicate children's targets to reinforce communication. For instance, targets can be hung on walls in the form of posters, pictures or any other visual form in schools or at home. Children can also be reminded of their targets through conversations so that they have an opportunity to hear what is expected of them. This variety can increase the likelihood of the effective communication of targets.

Success through target-setting also requires effective monitoring strategies. Adults need to observe children to assess how much progress they make towards meeting their targets. Even small steps can be noticed and be communicated to children. Adults can find their own ways of monitoring progress, which also make sense to children. For instance, each time a child performs a positive step towards meeting an important target (e.g. doing homework at home, behaving positively) he or she can glue a sticker on a chart. When a certain level of achievement has been reached (e.g. as measured by the number of stickers), he or she can be rewarded for his or her success. It is also important to recognise and praise the children's effort as well as what has been achieved.

SUMMARY

In this chapter we explored a framework developed by Olsen and Cooper (2001), designed to analyse problem situations and identify opportunities for intervention. This framework has five key areas. These are **S**ystems, **A**ccess, **L**imits, **A**cceptance and **D**irection. The framework is based on the idea that behavioural difficulties often stem from problems in the relationships between parents, children and schools rather than from within individuals. An important objective of the SALAD framework is to identify patterns of interaction between people that create and/or keep problems going, and ways in which these patterns might be altered.

- The **S** in SALAD refers to 'Systems'. 'Systems' emphasise the crucial notion that what goes on in the two-person subsystem has an influence on and is influenced by other relationships. It further outlines a framework for analysing problem situations effectively through defining and re-framing, as well as encouraging different parties (e.g. carers, teachers and the child) to work towards common goals to improve problem situations.

- The **A** in SALAD refers to 'Access'. 'Access' points out that the child needs to have access to knowledge of what behaviour and behavioural standards are expected of him or her. Key to the development of this kind of awareness is increasing students' *ownership* of their behaviour, including problem situations and their solutions.

- The **L** in SALAD refers to 'Limits'. 'Limits' can be thought of as behavioural boundaries. A boundary is a line that should not be crossed, because to cross it is to produce undesirable consequences for everyone involved. Communication of limits and boundaries is very important since they help children to regulate their own behaviour.

- The **A** in SALAD refers to 'Acceptance'. Acceptance relates to the notion of being welcomed as a member of a social circle. The opposite of acceptance is 'rejection'.

- The **D** in SALAD refers to 'Direction'. 'Direction' refers to guiding and scaffolding children for improvement. Overall, setting and communicating limits, boundaries, expectations and targets help children to regulate their own behaviour towards desired behaviour.

CHAPTER 9

What makes a Successful Nurture Group?

In previous chapters, we have explored what nurture groups are and how they function. We also reported on research evidence that illuminates the philosophy and organisational structure of successful nurture groups. In this chapter, we further explore issues that contribute to the effectiveness of nurture groups. We pay particular attention to the collaborative responsibilities of each of the key stakeholders involved in nurture groups.

Immediate factors that contribute to success of a nurture group are: nurture group composition; attitudes of nurture group staff; the quality of support provided to students; teaching and learning in nurture groups; and the relationship between the nurture group teacher and the teaching assistant (Cooper and Tiknaz 2005; Cooper, Arnold and Boyd 1999). The overall school support, the compatibility of the nurture group and the school ethos and values, the perceptions and support of mainstream staff, and headteacher backing are other crucial factors that affect the success of groups. Beyond school boundaries, carers also have an important role to play to support the children's progress and extend nurture group work to home. Committees that are set up to oversee the functioning of several nurture groups (i.e. steering committees), as well as the professional development opportunities available for staff, could further influence the effectiveness of nurture groups. Figure 9.1 illustrates these interacting factors.

FACTORS OPERATING IN NURTURE GROUPS
Nurture group composition

A balanced group composition appears to be a crucial factor in successful nurture groups. Balance is important because a nurture group is a small setting, and how the individual students in the group gel together, and how they respond to

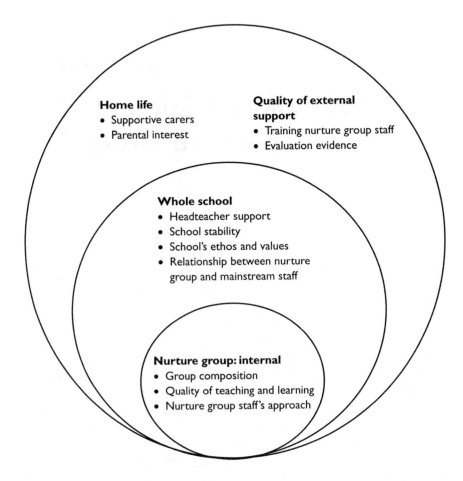

Figure 9.1: Nurture group success – the big picture

each other and to the staff, are important factors influencing the quality of relationships. For these reasons, nurture group staff are expected to give careful consideration to the selection of children for nurture group placement.

It is also important that nurture group staff pay great attention to the need to establish a balance in terms of the nature of problems presented by students in the group, as well as gender, age and achievement level. As discussed in Chapter 5, there are a number of tools (e.g. the Boxall Profile and the Goodman Strengths and Difficulties Questionnaire) that are used to select students for nurture groups. These tools are used by school staff to help define the nature of each student's needs.

When there is an overabundance of students with acting-out behaviours, the nurture group staff spend excessive amounts of time calming them down and managing the disruptive behaviour, which prevents them from creating a supportive environment for everyone in the nurture group (Cooper and Tiknaz 2005).

Gender balance is also considered to be important for the successful running of a nurture group. An equal representation of boys and girls is usually preferred. When one gender is over-represented, there are risks for students in the under-represented group, who may feel isolated. Research suggests that when one gender is under-represented, nurture group staff need to ensure the students in the under-represented group attend the group at the same time, to avoid feelings of isolation (Unpublished Nurture Group Evaluation Report, 2003).

Balance in nurture groups is also sought in terms of students' age range, though it is very common to find students from different year groups in the same nurture group. The issue of balance, in this regard, reflects the need to avoid having any one age group dominate the group in terms of numbers. It should be noted that this situation can be challenging for some students, who might experience problems adjusting to being in a group with students from a higher or lower year group (Unpublished Nurture Group Evaluation Report, 2001). However, at the same time, older students might provide role-models for younger ones, and may play a supportive and caring role, contributing to nurturing of the younger children (*ibid.*).

The relationship between nurture group teacher and the teaching assistant

An effective working partnership is one of the most crucial factors affecting the quality of support in nurture groups. The nurture group teacher and the teaching assistant (TA) have key roles in maintaining continuity and stability of the group. Ongoing effective communication involving joint understanding of the key principles of the group and what it wants to achieve are musts. This also implies clarity of their respective roles and responsibilities, and consideration of each other's needs. However, although roles should be clearly defined, there is also the need for staff to be flexible and willing to adjust what they do in response to the evolving needs of the individuals and the group. This may mean, therefore, that roles will change over time.

Earlier, we explored the specific roles and responsibilities of nurture group teachers and TAs. The relationship between the TA and the teacher in a nurture group is very distinctive. The two adults consciously engage in role-modelling appropriate communication skills. There is usually a tendency to avoid *hierarchical* relationships between teacher and TA, as well as a willingness to be *flexible*, and to work co-operatively. For instance, at different times the TA may be encouraged to prepare and deliver parts of teaching sessions. Or, if there is a differentiated lesson, the nurture group teacher and the TA can work with two separate groups of students, each adult instructing on different topics. Thus the TA's responsibilities in nurture groups are not limited to the domestic work, or to keeping children engaged with lessons being delivered by the teacher, as they might be in some mainstream classrooms. Rather, in the nurture group, TAs actively collaborate with the teacher in the planning of teaching sessions, and the support of children during sessions.

In effective nurture groups, the atmosphere of the group is highly dependent on the relationship between nurture group staff and nurture group children. This is often characterised by a sense of personal warmth, both between the two adults and between the adults and children (Cooper and Tiknaz 2005). The establishment of affectionate bonds between staff and students often flows from this atmosphere of personal warmth. The staff members actively and explicitly care for their students' well-being. As a result students learn to care for others and to appreciate others' needs.

THE EFFECTS OF THE BROADER SCHOOL ENVIRONMENT ON THE SUCCESS OF NURTURE GROUPS

The ultimate success of a nurture group is dependent on its being an integral part of the wider school community. From students' point of view, the nurture group needs to be seen as simply one facility within the school, just like the gymnasium or the music room or any other classroom. The nurture group should certainly not be the only place in the school where 'nurturing' approaches are used. The literature on schools with nurture groups often uses terms such as: 'nurturing schools', 'caring schools' (Unpublished Nurture Group Evaluation Report, 2002; Unpublished Nurture Goup Evaluation Report, 2003), or 'nurturing school ethos'. It is clearly the case that effective nurture groups are found in nurturing schools. As noted in Chapter 3, these different views are often expressed as to whether successful nurture groups create nurturing schools, or whether nurture groups become successful because of the support they receive from nurturing schools. It is probably the case that the influence is two-way. Schools with a nurturing ethos are likely to be instrumental in promoting the success of nurture groups, whilst the nurture group itself helps to develop and extend the school's ability to provide a nurturing environment.

It is important that nurture groups should be welcomed by school staff from the outset and supported by the school community. This is a vital factor for the survival and success of nurture groups. In order to achieve this, headteachers, mainstream teachers and nurture group staff have specific responsibilities to fulfil.

Effective communication between different stakeholders is important and, in the following, we describe the role each stakeholder can play in this process.

Communication between nurture group and mainstream staff

This section highlights some of the ways which nurture group staff and mainstream staff can work well together. The recognition of respective roles and responsibilities, effective communication, and the sharing of values and understandings relating to the purposes of nurture groups are important in making this collaborative partnership work.

Respective roles and responsibilities for building an effective working partnership

Responding to the needs of nurture group students cannot be left solely in the hands of nurture group staff. Mainstream staff play a crucial role in creating a whole school nurturing environment. In the nurturing school, all staff show awareness of students' emotional needs and are able and willing to provide appropriate forms of support (Postlethwaite and Hackney 1988).

Nurture group staff have a key role to play in sharing their expertise in supporting children with social, emotional and behavioural needs with mainstream colleagues. Appropriately trained nurture group staff will have specialist theoretical understanding and expertise in meeting children's psychological needs. This draws attention to the importance of the quality of the communication that takes place between nurture group and mainstream staff.

In successful nurturing schools, nurture group and mainstream staff share information about students' specific needs and the strategies that can be used to meet these needs. They will also share resources. In successful nurture groups, nurture group staff communicate regularly with mainstream staff about the progress of individual students. This sometimes takes the form of a written record that is passed to the mainstream teacher when the nurture group student returns to the mainstream class. This record may give an indication of a student's emotional state, or describe an incident that has involved the student. This information can then be used to inform the class teacher's handling of the student on that day. In turn, the mainstream staff also record similar information and pass this to the nurture group staff. This constant communication helps the staff to monitor students' progress and creates another opportunity for staff to collaborate.

Nurture group and mainstream staff share key responsibilities for supporting students' academic progress. Nurture group and mainstream staff should work in a co-ordinated way to ensure that each student receives a broad and balanced curriculum. Both sets of staff need to collaborate on key decisions about students' academic, social and emotional progress.

Tensions between mainstream teachers and nurture group teachers

Research evidence indicates that tensions can occur between mainstream and nurture group staff when communication is infrequent and lacking in quality (Cooper and Tiknaz 2005). This is often associated with a lack of clarity about each other's roles and respective objectives. Other factors that can slow down and decrease the efficiency of nurture groups are:

- nurture group staff taking ownership of the nurture group student
- nurture group staff perceiving the mainstream staff solely as the deliverer of the academic curriculum
- mainstream staff seeing the nurture group as a non-academic setting
- nurture group staff devaluing the skills of other staff and carers and blaming others for students' difficulties
- mainstream staff perceiving the nurture group as a sin bin
- negative perceptions towards the cost of nurture group provision (e.g. the employment of two adults for 10–12 students).

Having identified the nature of potential problems, the following section outlines a number of suggestions on how to facilitate good communication between nurture group and mainstream staff.

Facilitating communication between nurture group and mainstream staff

As Table 9.1 shows, the partnership between nurture group and mainstream staff is a specific one and the feedback interaction between them does not only convey information on what happened in the past. Ideally, this interaction should lead to an action plan to support students and meet their needs. Planning together for constructive action is a very important dimension of communication between nurture group and mainstream staff.

In addition to what the nurture group staff and the mainstream staff communicate, the way they communicate affects the quality of this working partnership. As Table 9.1 indicates, they need to be prepared to listen to each other in a non-judgemental way and be mutually approachable. They should be able to *understand* each other, *share* an action plan and *motivate* each other about what they can do together. Of course, success should be celebrated together.

Table 9.1: Facilitating communication between nurture group and mainstream staff

	Nurture group staff	Mainstream staff
Personal qualities	• Being approachable. • Appreciating difficulties and concerns experienced by the mainstream staff. • Being an effective communicator. • Willing and ready to collaborate. • Avoiding blame.	• Being approachable. • Appreciating difficulties and concerns experienced by the nurture group staff. • Willing and ready to collaborate. • Avoiding blame.
Professional qualities	• Be ready to share information about students' needs and academic progress. • Share student targets that are set in nurture groups. • Offer regular feedback on what is being done in the nurture group. • Be willing to offer explanations why things are done as they are in the nurture group. • Develop communication tools (e.g. special logs and notebooks). • Develop joint strategies to maximise support for the nurture group student (e.g. reintegration to mainstream classroom).	• Be ready to share information about students' needs and academic progress in the mainstream classroom. • Share student targets that are set in the mainstream classroom. • Offer regular feedback on what is being done in the mainstream classroom. • Be willing to learn from the nurture group staff and allow them to be influenced by the mainstream classroom.
Appropriate interaction	• Actively listen to each other. • Attack problems and issues rather than students and each other. • Care about and respect each other's work. • Maintain effective professional communication. • Provide specific information about how children can be supported throughout different stages of their nurture group experience.	

Research evidence suggests that communication is an area for improvement for the large majority of nurture groups. Even in some schools where there are highly successful nurture groups, mainstream staff highlight the need for improved communication with nurture group staff. Building on the current research reviews on nurture groups and the ideas of Wilkinson and Cave (1987), we suggest communication can be improved when staff:

- *select and prioritise* the needs of students who require attention. Raising too many issues may lead to a loss of focus and may prevent nurture group and mainstream staff from developing effective strategies to address students' needs

- *are sensitive* to each other's task and try to understand what each is trying to achieve

- *observe* each other's lessons. This is a valuable activity that promotes understanding and appreciation of each other's roles and responsibilities.

When nurture group staff spend time in mainstream classrooms, they commonly report that this helps to consolidate their relationship with nurture group students in that class. Nurture group students value this because it indicates their importance to the nurture group teacher. When mainstream teachers spend time in nurture groups, they often report that they gain valuable insights in engaging students with social, emotional and behavioural needs in the mainstream classrooms.

A whole school approach towards supporting nurture groups

Any successful whole school approach requires a proactive, constructive and consistent approach in supporting key values of the school (Derrington and Groom 2004). The success of nurture groups is often seen to be dependent on this kind of approach led by the headteacher's ability and willingness to show support for the nurture group and to articulate this in a way that locates the nurture groups at the heart of the values and purposes of the school as a whole.

To extend the whole school support in any policy or intervention, it should always be kept 'active' (Derrington and Groom 2004, p.2). When there is consistency between the school's key values and ethos and those of the nurture group, it is likely that the nurture group will be accepted and supported by the majority of school staff. For instance, in some schools, the key values which underpin the nurturing philosophy are very often in school policy documents, which mean that they are officially acknowledged as a guide to all members of the school community.

Good communication within school is vital to securing whole school support for the nurture group. School communities are more likely to become supportive if they fully understand:

- what a nurture group is
- why nurture groups are configured as they are
- the reasons why the nurture group is needed specifically in this school
- what the nurture group is intended to achieve
- the time scale for the group's functioning
- how the group functions
- what the mainstream staff need to do to support the nurture group.

Poor communication of the above issues can raise important tensions. Poor communication may also mean the loss of school resources. Misunderstood policies, unclear objectives and inaccurate or too little information can cause delays and inefficiency (Trethowan 1985).

Patterns of communication are intimately related to a school's atmosphere or 'ethos'. Open and honest communication is more likely to exist when people have good relationships and trust one another (Wilkinson and Cave 1987). On the other hand, good relationships and trust can only emerge when there is good communication. These factors are also associated with high morale and confidence among staff. Headteachers have a major task in leading their schools in ways that they create a school climate that promotes clear and positive lines of communication. This, in turn, is likely to lead to the development of a supportive environment for nurture groups.

Stability of the nurture group

The stability of school also appears to be a factor in running successful nurture groups. Stability of the nurture group is dependent upon having consistent staffing. Changes in staffing in the middle of a year, for example, could have a seriously disruptive effect on nurture groups and lead to students feeling unsettled. The important process of interpersonal bonding that is central to the success of nurture groups takes a considerable amount of time to develop. Any interruption to this process will have a detrimental effect on the effectiveness of the group. Other factors external to the group, for example changes in key staff such as the headteacher, can have a negative effect on the nurture group, again creating a sense of instability.

OUT OF SCHOOL FACTORS AFFECTING SUCCESSFUL RUNNING OF NURTURE GROUPS
Developing a working partnership with carers

> Children's progress will be diminished if their parents are not seen as partners in the educational process with unique knowledge to impart. Professional help can seldom be effective unless it builds on parents' capacity to be involved and unless parents consider that professionals take account of what they say and treat their views and anxieties as intrinsically important. (DfE 1994, p.12).

In this section, we start with two assumptions about the roles of carers in relation to nurture groups. First, the fullest involvement of carers in their child's educational experience is in the best interest of the child. Second, we recognise the ability of carers to enrich their children's personal and educational development. The problem is that most carers are unaware that their contribution to their children's abilities is so powerful (Freeman and Gray 1989).

Parental involvement is extremely important to the success of nurture group provision. When children are assessed for nurture group placements, the information that carers can provide is crucial and influential. It is important that carers are encouraged to recognise the value of their knowledge and the impact that it can have in supporting school staff (Postlethwaite and Hackney 1988). Also, if carers are motivated they can participate in supporting the nurture group with their own resources.

Following from the assumptions that we make at the beginning of this section, we will explore the importance of parental involvement and its potential benefits in supporting the nurture group. In order to do this, first we will explore what carers and nurture group staff expect from each other respectively. Then we will illustrate potential barriers which prevent a working partnership developing between carers and nurture group staff, before offering solutions on how to facilitate effective communication and resolve potential conflicts.

What might carers expect from nurture group staff?

Carers need effective communication not only with the nurture group staff but with all of the school staff who work with their children. We believe that it is largely the professional's responsibility to facilitate effective communication.

What carers expect from a nurture group may change throughout their children's experience in the group. In the initial stages, carers may have concerns and need specific information about what nurture groups are, and how their children are assessed and selected for this provision. Furthermore, they will want to know what their children do in the nurture group and the ways in which it differs from mainstream classrooms. The communication of this information is crucial since some carers may feel apprehensive about their child's temporary separation from their mainstream classrooms.

Throughout the later stages of children's experience in nurture groups, carers may want information on their child's progress. They will want to know about their child's strengths and difficulties, in terms of their social, emotional and behavioural progress, as well as their, it is to be hoped, evolving academic attainment. In the later stages, carers will be interested in how their child copes with his or her return to the mainstream classroom. Lastly, carers may appreciate guidance from teachers on how to promote their children's progress at home (Hornby 1995).

What might nurture group staff expect from carers?

Nurture group staff might expect a certain *commitment* from carers. The nurture group is a special provision and, as already noted, stability is crucial for the group to function successfully. The group's stability is related not only to the stability of nurture group staff, but also to the stability in terms of students' attendance. Without regular child attendance, it would be very difficult for the staff to develop and sustain a positive relationship with students to create a nurturing classroom.

Commitment can also be associated with carers' other responsibilities, such as bringing their child to school *on time*. In previous chapters, we highlighted the importance of the first minutes of the nurture group classrooms in the morning. During this brief period nurture group staff can prepare students for what will come and help them to put their worries and emotional baggage away. Missing such a crucial stage of a nurture group day not only results in the child missing out on a positive opportunity, but it also may cause the nurture group staff to feel frustrated.

It is essential that nurture group staff strive to establish a good quality relationship with carers. There will be times when the staff will benefit from having information about the child's home life. For instance, staff may want to know how the child reacts in his or her family situation; how the child gets on with her or his brothers or sisters (if any) and/or with their friends out of the school environment; how the child approaches his or her homework; and any changes in the child's attitudes towards school. Such information could add value to the nurture group staff's work by providing them with insightful information and another monitoring opportunity for potential improvements or deteriorations of the child's progress in needed areas. However, unless carers feel welcomed and respected, they are unlikely to be willing to reveal such personal information.

Barriers to the development of an effective partnership between carers and nurture group staff

The relationship between carers and the school community needs to be managed with care. An important issue here is the way in which school staff present themselves professionally. Professionalism is often equated with expertise. It is of course important that school staff are seen by carers as being competent professionals with expert knowledge. However, it is easy for expertness to become a mystifying cloak that discourages outside scrutiny of the expert's work. If this happens in the nurture group situation, then carers may feel intimidated and unwilling to make enquiries or, worse, to feel empowered to help with the process of educating their child. This *expert model* creates barriers between professionals and non-professionals (Cunningham and Davis 1985).

A more positive professional approach that is suitable for nurture group work is one which is characterised by the openness of the professional and his or her willingness to negotiate with the non-professional on equal terms. This is referred to as the *transplant* model (Cunningham and Davis 1985). With this approach, carers are seen as having rights, and the professional is seen as someone who facilitates the non-professional's ability to make good choices. In the case of nurture groups, these choices are often to do with appropriate methods of child rearing. In this type of professional–non-professional relationship, the communication channels are two-way and always open and the non-professional is empowered by the relationship, rather than being intimidated.

SUMMARY

In this chapter attention was given to key factors that contribute to the success of nurture groups. We considered factors that are within the nurture group, factors in the school beyond the nurture group, and factors outside the school. The complexity of the nurture group context is such that there are always going to be challenges to overcome. Particular emphasis is placed on the importance of communication between the various stakeholders and the need for roles and responsibilities to be clearly defined, but flexible.

CHAPTER 10

Key Messages for the Practitioner

The central concern of this book has been to explore the ways in which pupils with social, emotional and behavioural difficulties can be effectively engaged in schooling. We have shown that the social and emotional underpinnings of learning are vital to this process of engagement. We have also shown some of the practical strategies that exploit an understanding of these underpinnings that can be used by practitioners. This final chapter highlights some of the key messages of the book.

THE CHILD'S NEEDS ARE PARAMOUNT

When children present social, emotional and behavioural difficulties, they do so for good reasons. Children do not enjoy being regarded as 'difficult' or 'troublesome'. Social, emotional and behavioural difficulties are often the outward display of other problems. In this way the troubled or troublesome child communicates their stress and discomfort through their undesirable behaviour.

The central role of carers and school staff is to promote every child's emotional and social well-being, as well as their cognitive and academic development. Unfortunately, there are times when pressures that are external to the staff–student/carer–child relationships interfere in ways that affect children in negative ways. For example, school staff struggle with the demands of the National Curriculum and the testing agenda, and carers may experience family and/or employment difficulties. These interferences may lead to the inadvertent neglect of the individual child's needs. It is vital therefore that staff and carers are vigilant and able to detect problems of this kind and intervene in ways such as those suggested in this book to protect and nurture the child.

THE IMPORTANCE OF NURTURING

This book has shown that nurture groups represent a successful, practical and increasingly widely used approach to educating students with social, emotional and behavioural difficulties. Nurture groups work because they provide a structured approach to meeting children's needs that is based on sound psychological and pedagogical principles. The effectiveness of nurture groups has also been established through rigorous evaluation studies. However, it would be a mistake to assume that educational nurturing can only take place within a nurture group. Whilst there may always be a need among some children for access to a nurture group, the needs of all children will be better served by the adoption of nurturing values, attitudes and approaches in all educational settings, including the family.

THE IMPORTANCE OF TEACHING ASSISTANTS

Throughout the book we have repeatedly highlighted the central role of the relationship between teacher and teaching assistant (TA). Teaching and nurturing in nurture groups are group activities in which TAs play a crucial role. TAs have a direct contribution to make to pupils' social and academic engagement. They help increase pupils' opportunities to gain access to the school curriculum, and also help to manage social engagement activities by providing role models and interaction opportunities for pupils.

The emphasis throughout has been on the relationship between staff in the nurture group setting. This draws attention to potential dangers associated with the assignment of individual TAs to specific pupils, which is a practice adopted in some schools. There is strong evidence to suggest that such one-to-one attachments can sometimes have negative consequences for pupils in that the TA can become a barrier between the pupil and the learning experience (Cajkler *et al.* 2006). Also, this relationship can be experienced as stigmatising, especially at the secondary level. We argue very strongly, therefore, that the interactive model of TA–teacher functioning modelled in nurture groups offers a framework that would be beneficial to almost any educational setting. TAs have an increasingly important pedagogic role that is often both complementary to and distinctive from that of the teacher (Cajkler *et al.* 2006).

Central to the effective TA role is the function of mediation. TAs will often be drawn from the same communities as the children attending a school (Roaf 2003). This gives the TA insight into the lives of children that may not be readily available to other school staff. In some cases, the TA's local knowledge may be a valuable resource to the school in helping to understand how community issues may impact on life in the school. On the other hand, from the pupil's perspective, this familiarity may help to make the school environment easier to relate to. The TA can also act as a link person by maintaining relationships between different stakeholders, for example between parents and schools (in some cases as a cross-cultural link), and bridging between teachers and pupils, for example listening to pupil perspectives and feeding back to teachers (Cajkler *et al.* 2006).

NURTURING AND PROFESSIONAL DEVELOPMENT

We hope you have enjoyed reading this book. If we have been successful, we have in some cases helped widen your knowledge and understanding of the needs of children with social, emotional and behavioural difficulties, and have added to your stock of ideas about what might be done to increase schools', teachers' and parents' abilities to meet these needs. Also, we hope that the book has stimulated readers to reflect on their own experience and practice. We consider this process of reflection to be a vital stage in the process of professional development. However, reflection alone is only part of this process.

Reflection on practice can on the one hand help to reassure professionals that their practice is appropriate. On the other hand, it may result in the identification of the need for change. There is a great deal that the professional can do to promote change in their practice simply by thinking about their experiences and devising and testing hypotheses. But this process will often be enhanced when the professional shares their reflections with other people. This can take the form of informal interaction with colleagues or interaction with colleagues in more formal settings such as planning sessions and staff meetings, or it can take place on professional development courses.

There are now many opportunities for school staff to receive formal accredited training in the theory of practice of nurture groups, as well as other aspects of work with children with social, emotional and behavioural difficulties in the UK. Such training is vitally important because of the way in which it enables professionals to take a fresh look at practical classroom issues in the relatively un-pressurised environment of a professional development course. It is on such courses that professionals have the leisure to examine their practices and the thinking that underlies them. However, a training course can only stimulate thought that may translate into action. Training courses will be most effective when staff carry their learning back into their schools and use it as a focus for group reflection.

Nurture group training courses not only focus on nurture group-specific issues, but also range over a variety of topics which are of general interest and importance to schools and school staff. These include:

- the social and emotional underpinnings of learning
- the importance of an understanding of child development as a basis for curricula design and pedagogy

- the importance of the social and physical environment to the development of educational engagement

- the importance of interaction and collegiality between staff, with particular emphasis on the roles and functions of teachers and teaching assistants

- the role that the senior school managers play in helping to facilitate the success of initiatives such as nurture groups

- the need for attention to be given to the quality of interaction between schools and parents and the need for empathy in these relationships

- the importance of evidence-based practice and the use of observational techniques and psychometric measures

- positive behaviour management.

CARERS, TEACHERS AND STUDENTS NEED TO WORK TOGETHER: THE IMPORTANCE OF EMPATHY

Throughout the book, we have emphasised the values and strategies that are necessary to develop empathetic relationships between stakeholders. School staff need to empathise with their pupils and their pupils' carers. Carers need to be able to empathise with their children and their children's teachers and teaching assistants. And pupils need to learn to empathise with one another. Empathy is infectious. One of the best ways to get another person to empathise with us is for us to empathise with them. Put simply, empathy is the opposite to *blame*. Blame creates conflict and defensiveness, whilst empathy promotes constructive co-operation.

For nurture group staff, there are particular considerations in relation to the development of an empathic climate. There are certain features of nurture group work that can make it particularly challenging and stressful. The students that staff work with in the nurture group, by definition, present particular 'difficulties'. This means these are students who are deemed to present challenges that are above and beyond what can be adequately managed in the mainstream classroom. On the other hand, to the ill-informed observer it may appear that the nurture group staff have an easy life, with 12 or fewer students, in a well-equipped and customised classroom. It is important therefore that mainstream staff are encouraged to recognise not only the important service that the nurture group provides to its pupils and the school as a whole, but also the particular challenges that the nurture group staff face on a day-to-day basis.

And finally...

This has been a book concerned with what at first might appear to be a rather depressing topic. The distress of students with social, emotional and behavioural difficulties can be harrowing to observe. However, the central message of this book is a positive one. Students with social, emotional and behavioural difficulties do not have to be condemned to lives of misery and educational failure. The more we understand about what lies behind the difficulties that the children present, the better placed we are to engage with them in positive ways. The good news is that all of the ideas in this book are based on what is actually happening in some schools as we write. Our hope for the future is that more schools will adopt these approaches.

APPENDIX
Introducing the Nurture Group Network

It is with great pleasure that I write this appendix, as the content of this most informative and well-written book emphasises and demonstrates through evidence-based approaches the powerful effect that nurture groups have, not only on the lives of individual children, but also on families and whole school communities. Such a perspective is essential as it is almost impossible to think about meeting the needs of vulnerable children without thinking about their family situation and the significant relationships that are critical for healthy growth and positive emotional development.

In its role as the national umbrella organisation for nurture groups, the Nurture Group Network sets out its key aims and priorities thus:

> The Nurture Group Network exists to promote nurture groups as an effective way of meeting the needs of vulnerable children and to ensure the continuing quality of their delivery through accredited training programmes, relevant publications, research and information exchange.

The Nurture Group Network was formally constituted in 2003 as an autonomous division of the long standing and highly regarded charity, SEBDA (Social, Emotional and Behavioural Difficulties Association). This followed a number of years of effort by a largely volunteer workforce who, under the inspired leadership of Marion Bennathan, had established what was then known as the Nurture Group Consortium as a national organisation involved with training and research in nurture group work. In June 2004 the Nurture Group Network Executive Committee took the decision to separate from SEBDA and to establish the Network as a company limited by guarantee with charitable status.

The work of the Nurture Group Network has expanded enormously over recent years to the point where in January 2004 an appointment was made for the first salaried director and in May 2005 a part-time national training manager was also appointed to the team.

The scale of this growth is best represented through considering the organisation's core activities as set out in the mission statement.

TRAINING

From the early days of the Consortium the provision of high quality training has been a priority and its availability to staff engaged in nurture group work has been an important factor in raising the standards of nurture group work and ensuring effectiveness in delivery.

Perhaps the most exciting innovation has been the development by the Network of the Certificate Course in partnership with the University of Leicester. This course, designated 'The Theory and Practice of Nurture Group Work', can now be delivered by the Nurture Group Network to local authority staff in their own location, offering the flexibility to reflect upon and respond to local issues and needs.

CONFERENCES

Another important way of promoting the message about nurture groups is through the programme of conferences organised on both a regional and national basis. Conferences also allow for focusing on crucial aspects of nurture group work such as the involvement of parents and carers. In October 2004 a conference entitled 'Supporting Parents, Supporting Education: What Nurture Groups Achieve' attracted an audience of over 80 people to Stirling University. A publication, including a full write-up of this conference, is now available from the Nurture Group Network.

In September 2005 over 100 people attended a national conference in London on 'Nurture Groups with Older Children, Too Little Too Late or Better Late Than Never?'. With input from the Department for Education and Skills and the Youth Justice Board this conference addressed the growing interest in how nurture group principles may be applied to working situations with adolescents.

PUBLICATIONS

The Nurture Group Network remains the sole distributor of the *Boxall Profile Handbook*, the key diagnostic tool for supporting nurture group staff in understanding more about the emotional and developmental needs of the children with whom they are working. The other standard texts on nurture group work are:

- Bennathan, M. and Boxall, M. (2000) *Effective Intervention in Primary Schools: Nurture Groups*, 2nd edn. London: David Fulton.

- Boxall, M. (2002) *Nurture Groups in School: Principles and Practice.* London: Paul Chapman.

MEMBERSHIP SERVICES

With over 400 individuals and 200 schools joining the Network, membership is organised on a regional basis with a number of regions holding regular support meetings. Services to members have been greatly improved by the redesigning of the website, the new version of which was launched in June 2005, and the revamping of the quarterly newsletter into a magazine, *Nurture*, published each school term. Both of these initiatives have given greater scope for keeping members informed about nurture group developments as well as presenting a stronger image of the Network's work to a wider audience.

An extensive consultation has taken place with regard to the introduction of the Marjorie Boxall Quality Mark Award. Along with a more focused training programme the introduction of this quality assurance scheme will go a considerable way to addressing the long-term problem of ensuring consistency in the quality of nurture group provision and in maintaining the integrity of the model to the benefit of children across the UK.

RESEARCH

Encouraging and promoting research activity has always been integral to the nurture group approach and the national research programme led by Paul Cooper provides the most comprehensive account to date of the effectiveness of nurture groups. It is interesting to note how the outcomes of the research show the effectiveness of nurture groups not only in the improvements made by individual children but on the impact that they make across whole school communities and families.

What happens with school, that is attending regularly, achieving reasonably well, making friends, is one of the most powerful factors in ensuring a child's healthy development and emotional well-being. And so, in conclusion, I commend this book and the contribution that it makes in increasing our understanding about nurture groups and the invaluable part they can play in helping children and families get the best out of the exciting opportunities that come from good experiences of education and school.

Jim Rose, Director
The Nurture Group Network
www.nurturegroups.org

References

Bateson, G. (1972) *Steps to an Ecology of Mind.* New York: Chandler.

Bennathan, M. and Boxall, M. (1998) *The Boxall Profile: A Guide to Effective Intervention in the Education of Pupils with Emotional and Behavioural Difficulties.* East Sutton, Maidstone: Association of Workers for Children with Emotional and Behavioural Difficulties.

Bennathan, M. and Boxall, M. (2000) *Effective Intervention in Primary Schools: Nurture Groups,* 2nd edn. London: Fulton.

Bishop, A. and Swain, J. (2000a) 'Early years education and children with behavioural and emotional difficulties: nurturing parental involvement.' *Emotional and Behavioural Difficulties 5,* 4, 26–31.

Bishop, A. and Swain, J. (2000b) 'The bread, the jam and some coffee in the morning: peceptions of a nurture group.' *Emotional and Behavioural Difficulties 5,* 3, 18–23.

Bodrova, E. and Leong, D.J. (1998) 'Adult Influences on Play: the Vygotskian Approach.' In D.P. Fromberg and D. Began (eds) *Play from Birth to Twelve and Beyond: Context, Perpectives and Meanings.* New York: Garland Publishing.

Boorn, C. (2002) 'Locating a nurture group: identifying and evaluating features within a school that would make a suitable host.' Unpublished MSc thesis, University of Sheffield.

Bowlby, J. (1969) *Attachment and Loss.* London: Penguin.

Bowlby, J. (1980) *Attachment and Loss,* vol. 13, *Loss: Sadness and Depression.* London: Penguin.

Boxall, M. (2002) *Nurture Groups in School: Principles and Practice.* London: Paul Chapman.

British Medical Association (2006) *Child and Adolescent Mental Health – A Guide for Healthcare Professionals.* London: BMA.

Broadhead, P. and English, C. (1994) 'Open-ended Role Play: Supporting Creativity and Developing Identity.' In J. Moyles (ed.) *The Excellence of Play.* Milton Keynes: Open University Press.

Bruner, J. and Haste, H. (1987) *Making Sense: The Child's Construction of the World.* London: Methuen.

Cajkler, W., Tennant, G., Cooper, P. W., Sage, R., Tansey, R., Taylor, C., Tucker, S.A. and Tiknaz, Y. (2006) *A Systematic Literature Review on the Perceptions of Ways in which Support Staff Work to Support Pupils' Social and Academic Engagement in Primary Classrooms (1988–2003).* London: The EPPI-Centre, Social Science Research Unit, Institute of Education, University of London.

Cooper, P. (1993) *Effective Schools for Disaffected Students.* London: Routledge.

Cooper, P. (2005) 'Is inclusion just a buzz-word?' *Emotional and Behavioural Difficulties 9,* 4, 219–222.

Cooper, P. and Lovey, J. (1999) 'Early intervention in emotional and behavioural difficulties: the role of NGs.' *European Journal of Special Needs Education 14,* 2, 122–131.

Cooper, P. and MacIntyre, D. (1996) *Effective Teaching and Learning: Teachers' and Students' Perspectives.* Buckingham: Open University Press.

Cooper, P. and Tiknaz, Y. (2004) 'The evaluation of nurture groups in Braunstone.' Second interim research report, University of Leicester, Centre for Innovation in Raising Educational Achievement.

Cooper, P. and Tiknaz, Y. (2005) 'Progress and challenge in nurture groups: evidence from three case studies.' *British Journal of Special Education 32*, 4, 211–223.

Cooper, P. and Upton, G. (1990) 'An ecosystemic approach to emotional and behavioural problems in schools.' *Educational Psychology 10*, 4, 301–321.

Cooper, P. and Whitebread, D. (2007) 'The effectiveness of nurture groups on student progress: evidence from a national research study'. *Emotional and Behavoural Difficulties 12*, 3, (in press). Leicester, School of Education.

Cooper, P., Arnold, R. and Boyd, E. (1998) *The Nature and Distribution of Nurture Groups in England and Wales.* Cambridge: University of Cambridge School of Education.

Cooper, P., Arnold, R. and Boyd, E. (1999) *The Nature and Distribution of NGs in England and Wales.* Cambridge: University of Cambridge School of Education.

Cooper, P., Arnold, R. and Boyd, E. (2000) 'The rise and rise of nurture groups.' *School of Education Newsletter 6*, Summer 2000, University of Cambridge.

Coplan, R.J. and Rubin, K.H. (1998) 'Social Play.' In D.P. Fromberg and D. Began (eds) *Play from Birth to Twelve and Beyond: Contexts, Perspectives and Meanings.* New York: Garland Publishing.

Cunningham, C.C. and Davis, H. (1985) *Working with Parents: Frameworks for Collaboration.* Buckingham: Open University Press.

Dale, N. (1996) *Working with Families of Children with Special Educational Needs: Partnership And Practice.* London: Routledge.

Derrington, C. and Groom, B. (2004) *A Team Approach to Behaviour Management: A Training Guide for SENCOs Working with Teaching Assistants.* London: Paul Chapman.

DfE (Department for Education) (1994) *Code of Practice on the Identification and Assessment of Special Educational Needs.* London: Department for Education.

Doyle, R. (2001) 'Using a readiness scale for reintegrating pupils with social, emotional and behavioural difficulties from a Nurture Group into their mainstream classroom: a pilot study.' *British Journal of Special Education 28*, 3, 126–132.

Ellis, H.C. and Ashbrook, P.W. (1988) 'Resource Allocation Model of the Effects of Depressed Mood States on Memory.' In K. Fielder and J. Forgas (eds) *Affect, Cognition, and Social Behaviour.* Toronto: Hogrefe.

Erikson, E.H. (1963) *Childhood and Society*, 2nd edn. New York: Norton.

Eysenck, M.W. and Calvo, M. G. (1992) 'Anxiety and performance: the processing efficiency theory.' *Cognition and Emotion 6*, 409–434.

Eysenck, M.W. and Keane, M.T. (1995) *Cognitive Psychology: A Student's Handbook.* East Sussex: Psychology Press.

Freeman, A. and Gray, H. (1989) *Organizing Special Educational Needs: A Critical Approach.* London: Paul Chapman.

Goodman, R. (1997) 'The Strengths and Difficulties Questionnaire: a research note.' *Journal of Child Psychology and Psychiatry 38*, 581–586.

Goodman, R. (1999) 'The extended version of the Strengths and Difficulties Questionnaire as a guide to child psychiatric casess and consequent burden'. *Journal of Child Psuchology and Psychiatry 40*, 791–801.

Goodman, R. and Scott, S. (1999) 'Comparing the Strengths and Difficulties Questionnaire and the Child Behavior Checklist: Is small beautiful?' *Journal of Abnormal Child Psychology 27*, 17–24.

Hoffman, L. (1981) *Foundations of Family Therapy: A Conceptual Framework for Systems Change.* London: Basic Books.

Hornby, G. (1995) *Working with Parents of Children with Special Needs.* London: Cassell.

Iszatt, J. and Wasilewska, T. (1997) 'NGs: an early intervention model enabling vulnerable children with emotional and behavioural difficulties to integrate successfully into school.' *Educational and Child Psychology 14*, 3, 121–139.

Jones, R.A. (1995) *The Child–School Interface.* London: Cassell.

Kitson, N. (2006) 'Drama and Role-play in Learning.' In H. Carsch, Y. Tiknaz, P. Cooper and R. Sage (eds) *The Handbook of Social, Emotional and Behavioural Difficulties.* London: The Continuum Press.

Lucas, S. (1999) 'The nurturing school: the impact of NG principles and practice on the whole school.' *Emotional and Behavioural Difficulties 4*, 3, 14–19.

Maccoby, E.E. (1984) 'Middle Childhood in the Context of the Family.' In W.A. Collins (ed.) *Development and Childhood: The Years from Six to Twelve.* Washington, DC: National Academy of Science Press.

Maslow, A. (1970) *Motivation and Personality.* New York: Harper & Row.

Moyles, J.R. (1989) *Just Playing? The Role and Status of Play in Early Childhood Education.* Milton Keynes: Open University Press.

Nind, M. (1999) 'Intensive interaction and autism: a useful approach?' *British Journal of Special Education 26*, 2, 96–102.

Nourot, P.M. (1998) 'Sociodramatic Play: Pretending Together.' In D.P. Fromberg and D. Bergen, *Play from Birth to Twelve and Beyond: Contexts, Perspectives and Meanings.* New York: Garland Publishing.

Nurture Group Network [NGN] (2001) *Curriculum Guidelines for Nurture Groups 2001.* London: Nurture Group Network, The Association of Workers for Children with Emotional and Behavioural Difficulties.

O'Connor, T. and Colwell, J. (2002) 'Understanding nurturing practices – a comparison of the use of strategies likely to enhance self-esteem in nurture groups and normal classrooms.' *British Journal of Special Education 30*, 3, 119–124.

Oden, S. and Hall, J.A. (1998) 'Peer and Sibling Influences on Play.' In D.P. Fromberg and D. Began (eds) *Play from Birth to Twelve and Beyond: Contexts, Perspectives and Meanings.* New York: Garland Publishing.

Olsen, J. (1989) 'Red herrings and school refusal.' *Australian Journal of Family Therapy 10*, 196.

Olsen, J. (1997) *Working with Troubled Students.* Canberra: Author (self-published).

Olsen, J. and Cooper, P. (2001) *Dealing with Disruptive Students in the Classroom.* London: Kogan Page.

Patterson, G.R., Reid, J.B. and Dishion, T.J. (1992) *Anti-Social Boys: A Social Interaction Approach*, vol.4. Eugene, OR: Castalia.

Postlethwaite, K. and Hackney, A. (1988) *Organising the School's Responses: Special Needs in Mainstream Schools.* London: Macmillan Education.

Pringle, M.K. (1975) *The Needs of Children: A Personal Perspective.* London: Hutchinson Education.

Reynolds, S. and Kearney, M. (2007) 'The impact of nurture groups on the psychological, educational and behavioural well-being of Glasgow's children', paper presented at The British Psychological Society, Division of Educational and Child Psychology conference, Glasgow, 3–5 January 2007.

Roaf, C. (2003) 'Learning Support Assistants Talk About Inclusion.' In M. Nind, K. Sheehy and K. Simmons (eds) *Inclusive Education: Learners and Learning Contexts.* London: David Fulton.

Rutter, M. and Smith, D. (1995) *Psychosocial Disorders in Young People.* Chichester: Wiley.

Slade, P. (1995) *Child Play: Its Importance for Human Development.* London: Jessica Kingsley Publishers.

Smith, D. (2006) *School Experience and Delinquency at Ages 13 to 16.* Edinburgh: Centre for Law and Society, University of Edinburgh.

Tiknaz, Y. (2004) 'An investigation into the theory and practice of formative assessment in Key Stage 3 Geography.' Unpublished EdD thesis, University of Leicester.

Trethowan, D.M. (1985) *Communication in Schools.* London: Contemprint Limited.

Von Bertalanffy, L. (1968) *General System Theory.* New York: Brazillier.

Walker, H., Calvin, G. and Ramsey, E. (1995) *Antisocial Behaviour in School: Strategies and Best Practices.* Pacific Grove, CA: Brooks/Cole.

Wilkinson, C. and Cave, E. (1987) *Teaching and Managing: Inseparable Activities in Schools.* London: Croom Helm.

Williamson, P.A. and Silvern, S.B. (1984) 'Creative Dramatic Play and Language Comprehension.' In T.D. Yawkey and A.D. Pellegrini (eds) *Child's Play: Developmental and Applied.* New Jersey: Lawrence Erlbaum Association.

Winnicott, D. (1964) *The Family and Individual Development.* London: Tavistock.

Wood, E. and Attfield, J. (2005) *Play, Learning and the Early Childhood Curriculum,* 2nd edn. London: Sage.

Youngminds (1999) *Spotlight No. 1.* London: Youngminds.

Subject Index

Author Index